MORE SEATS DOWNSTAIRS

LEON
HAPPY BAKING

BY CLAIRE PTAK & HENRY DIMBLEBY

LEON

HAPPY BAKING

BY CLAIRE PTAK & HENRY DIMBLEBY

conran
OCTOPUS

CONTENTS

WELCOME TO LEON HAPPY BAKING

Leon was founded on the belief that food should both taste good and do you good. In this book, we hope to show that this can be the case even where it is often thought impossible—when cooking comfort food. The dishes you will find here look indulgent, may seem not so good for you, and taste like the kind of treats that normally come with a side helping of guilt. Yet many of the recipes are wheat, dairy, or refined sugar free, with plenty of vegan and gluten-free options.

We want this book to be accessible to even the most inexperienced cook— hence our Baking Basics section at the back on ingredients and techniques. Once you have mastered a recipe, you can use our suggested variations to put your own stamp on it. We also want to provide inspiration for the more experienced. Some of the recipes are daring (see Baked Alaska page 182), some draw on ancient wisdom (see Sourdough Bread page 21) and some are downright showstopping (see Leon's Birthday Cake page 126)—but even the more adventurous recipes shouldn't be that difficult for the careful amateur.

We hope this book finds a permanent place in your kitchen and becomes batter-smattered, tacky with caramel, and dog-eared through use.

Henry & Claire

KEY

WF
WHEAT FREE

GF
GLUTEN FREE

DF
DAIRY FREE

V
VEGETARIAN

Ve
VEGAN

BREADS

BREAD—THE BASICS

TYPES OF BREAD

All breads fall into four main categories, defined by what makes them rise:

SOURDOUGH

Sourdough is the most ancient form of leavened bread. It is made with a sourdough starter (see page 18), which can either be taken from someone else's existing starter or created by leaving wheat and water to ferment naturally. The starter contains a symbiotic combination of natural yeasts and lactobacillus culture. It is the culture that creates the lactic acid that gives this bread its distinctive sour taste.

Sourdough has a reputation for being frustrating and unpredictable if you don't make it all the time, because the starter needs attention. However, starters are surprisingly robust. Henry, being chaotic and absent minded, has had to bring many a forgotten and slimy starter back to life.

The thing that takes some getting used to is the timing. The cycle for making a loaf is a minimum of twelve hours and typically twenty-four. But the actual work involved is minimal (most of that time is spent waiting for the dough to rise), and the reward is a uniquely flavored loaf that stays fresh for more than a week.

YEASTED BREADS

Most bread is risen using baker's yeast, *Saccharomyces cerevisiae*. It is the same yeast that is used to brew alcohol. It feeds on the sugars in the wheat and converts them into carbon dioxide, the gas that causes the bread to rise. It is easier to use than a sourdough starter, because it does not require looking after and it is a good deal more vigorous—a loaf can rise in a couple of hours in a warm room. You can buy yeast fresh in cakes from specialty suppliers but it is much easier to find dried in granules.

If you have not made bread before, this is where to start. The spelt loaf on page 14 is outrageously easy to make and equally impressive. You can also experiment with different flour mixtures and flavorings to create your own signature loaf.

If you have some sourdough starter in the refrigerator, you can add a little to traditionally yeasted breads to get a touch of the flavor in under half the time.

SODA BREAD

This bread uses baking soda as its leavening agent. Wheat flour is mixed with buttermilk (or sometimes yogurt) and the lactic acid reacts with the soda to create bubbles of carbon dioxide, which raise the bread.

It is a relatively modern bread, having become popular in Ireland in the mid-nineteenth century as a cheaper and faster alternative to yeast. It has a wonderful soft, cakelike texture and a distinctive taste.

UNLEAVENED BREAD

This is a dough that requires no leavening agent at all. It is the easiest of all breads to make.

FLOUR STATION RYE BREAD

MAKES: 1 LARGE LOAF

PREP TIME: 1 HOUR + COOLING AND RISING · COOK TIME: 55 MINS–1 HOUR

WF · V (**DF · Ve** if oil is used for greasing)

2 tablespoons **rye flour starter**
(50:50 rye flour and water; see
Sourdough Starter on page 18)

butter or **oil,** for greasing

4 cups **rye flour,** plus extra for dusting

1 medium **potato**

1 cup lukewarm **water**

2 tablespoons **molasses**

¾ cup **sunflower seeds**

1 tablespoon (1½ envelopes)
active dry yeast

2 teaspoons **fine sea salt**

≡ TIP ≡

This bread actually improves with
age and is best enjoyed the day
after baking. It will stay fresh for at
least a week, as the potatoes attract
moisture and therefore keep the
bread moist for longer.

*This bread, which we use at Leon to make open sandwiches, is baked for
us by the magnificent bakers at London's Flour Station.*

First, make your starter according to the recipe on page 18, using rye flour.

Preheat the oven to 400°F. Grease a 9 x 5 x 3-inch loaf pan and dust it with rye flour.

Prick the skin of the potato and bake it in the oven for 1 hour. Let cool, then scoop
the flesh into a mixing bowl and mash until smooth. You need ¾ cup of potato.

Add the remaining ingredients to the bowl with the mashed potato, making sure the
yeast and salt don't make contact. Fit the bowl into a free-standing mixer fitted with
a dough hook and mix on a slow speed until all is well combined and a soft, sticky
dough has formed. You can do this by hand, too—just use a lot of elbow grease.

Transfer the dough onto a lightly floured surface, shape into a loaf, and put into
the prepared pan. Dust the top of the loaf with more rye flour, then cover the pan
with a damp dish towel and let rise in a warm place for about 12 hours (overnight is
easiest), until the dough has almost doubled in size. Preheat the oven to 425°F and
put a baking pan into the bottom of the oven to heat up. Fill a pitcher with scant
1 cup of water and have it ready.

Dust the loaf with rye flour again and place on the middle shelf of the oven. Quickly
pour the water into the baking pan, then immediately close the oven door—it will
create steam, which helps the bread develop a good crust. Bake for 55 minutes–
1 hour, until the loaf has a rich dark crust and sounds hollow when tapped on the
bottom. Turn out and cool on a wire rack.

SPELT BREAD

MAKES: 3 LOAVES

PREP TIME: 10 MINS + RISING · COOK TIME: 40 MINS

V (**DF · Ve** if oil is used for greasing)

butter or **oil**, for greasing

13⅓ cups **whole-grain spelt flour**

4½ teaspoons (2 envelopes) **instant yeast**

2 tablespoons **sea salt**, crushed

1 cup **pine nuts**

1 cup **pumpkin seeds**

1 cup **sunflower seeds**

½ cup **extra virgin olive oil**

3¾–4¼ cups warm **water**

⅓ cup **sunflower seeds** and **nuts**,
   to sprinkle

═ TIPS ═

These freeze really well in freezer bags, but don't keep bread in the refrigerator, because it turns stale more quickly.

You can use normal whole-wheat flour if you can't find spelt. Or for a lighter loaf, replace 4 cups of the whole-wheat flour with 3⅔ cups white bread flour.

Experiment with various additions. Breads with nuts and fruit can be amazing. Try date and almond, or apricot and walnut.

Add herbs and spices: rosemary, dill, and oregano are all interesting.

This is a bread that Henry has been baking for years, at his wife's insistence. It is especially easy to make and impossible to get wrong. It is also a great recipe to play with by adding nuts and seeds, mixing in spices, and using different flours.

Grease three 9 x 5 x 3-inch loaf pans.

Mix all the dry ingredients (except the seeds for the top) together in a bowl large enough to knead the dough in.

Add the oil, then the water, stirring until the mixture sticks together. Knead in the bowl for a few minutes, until smooth. You can add a little flour if it is too sticky, but remember the maxim: Wetter is better. It doesn't matter if a little of the dough sticks to your hands.

Cut into 3 pieces, shape into vague ovals, then put into the loaf pans. Cut a pattern of deep gashes on the top and sprinkle the seeds and nuts into the gashes, then sprinkle a little spelt flour (or bran if you have some on hand) all over.

Put the pans into large plastic food bags and tuck the ends of the bags under the pans, leaving them enclosed with plenty of air. Let stand until the dough has doubled in size. This will take about 2 hours in a warm kitchen.

Preheat the oven to 450°F. Bake the loaves for 20 minutes, then reduce the temperature to 400°F and bake for another 20 minutes. Turn out and cool on a rack.

RAAB THE BAKER'S CRUSTY WHITE ROLLS

MAKES: 10–12

PREP TIME: 30 MINS + RISING · COOK TIME: 20 MINS

V

⅔–1 cup warm **water**

1 packed tablespoon **fresh cake yeast**
or 2½ teaspoons **active dry yeast**

⅓ cup warm **milk**

a pinch of **sugar**

3¼ cups **white bread flour**

1 teaspoon **salt**

¼ cup packed **vegetable shortening**,
cut into cubes, or ¼ cup **vegetable oil**,
plus extra for greasing

handful of **ice cubes**

These crispy rolls are inspired by a family baker in Islington, London.

Put the water into a bowl, add the yeast, and stir to dissolve. Add the milk and a pinch of sugar to help activate the yeast.

Place the flour, salt, and shortening on a work surface, making a well in the middle (if using vegetable oil, add it in the next step).

Pour the liquid yeast mixture (and oil, if using) into the well and gradually blend it into the flour using your hands to form a dough. Add a little more flour to prevent sticking and knead for 10–12 minutes, until a smooth elastic dough is achieved.

Put the dough into a greased bowl, cover it with a damp dish towel, and let rest in a warm place for an hour, or until it has doubled in size.

Transfer the dough onto a floured work surface and divide it into 10–12 pieces. Shape them into rounds, pressing down with your hands in a circular motion.

Place the rolls on a lined or well-greased baking sheet, leaving enough room for the rolls not to touch once they have risen. Cut a slit in the top of each roll with a sharp knife. Cover with a dish towel.

Preheat the oven to 425°F and place an empty baking pan at the bottom of the oven. When the rolls have doubled in size, remove the dish towel and place the baking sheet in the oven. Throw the ice cubes onto the hot empty baking pan at the bottom of the oven (see tip). Bake the rolls for 15–20 minutes, until golden brown.

═ TIP ═

The ice cubes create steam, which is essential for a crusty roll.

SOURDOUGH STARTER

. . . .

DF · V · Ve (**WF** if you use rye flour)

. . . .

If you can't find a kindly soul to give you some starter, here are tips on how to make one, courtesy of master baker Tom Herbert, of Hobbs House Bakery in Gloucestershire, England. He gave Henry a piece of the starter that has been handed down in his family for 55 years.

. . . .

STARTING A SOURDOUGH

Find a suitable container to house your sourdough—a canning jar that has an airtight seal will be ideal. Make sure you clean it well.

Add 1 cup of organic whole-wheat, dark rye, or spelt flour (these all work really well) and ½ cup of warm water to your jar and stir. Put the jar into a prominent and warm place in your kitchen (this will be its second home), with the lid sealed.

Each day for a week repeat the feeding process. Put ½ cup of the starter into a bowl (take out the surplus and use to flavor cakes, buns, pancakes, and pizza dough), add ½ cup of water and 1 cup of flour, and stir vigorously to remove all floury lumps with a clean finger or a fork. Return it to the empty jar.

After about 5 days you'll notice bubbles in the dough—like the first burpy smile of a baby. You can start to use it after a week, but it'll be slow, weak, and infantile. From now on, you can keep it in the refrigerator (its first home), removing it a couple of days before use to feed it back into full bubbly liveliness (using ½ cup of starter, 1 cup of flour, and ½ cup of water as before).

After a month, the dough will have matured and you'll get a better, more even flavor and rising performance.

If it is not performing well enough, try taking it out of the refrigerator and giving it an extra feed. Remember that it is a living culture—if it's not hibernating in the refrigerator, where it can survive for several months—and it likes to be fed, kept warm, and aerated (stirred/whisked). You'll know if it dies, because it'll smell like a dead dog on a hot day. Throw out the whole thing and start again.

I'm the custodian of our family sourdough, which has been raising award-winning loaves at Hobbs House Bakery for more than 55 years. Who will you leave your sourdough to in your will?

Peace and loaf,

Tom Herbert

SOURDOUGH BREAD

MAKES: 1 LOAF

PREP TIME: 45 MINS + RISING · COOK TIME: 35–40 MINS

DF · V · Ve

SPONGE:

¾ cup **water** at about 80°F

½ cup **sourdough starter** (see page 18);
   brought to room temperature

2½ cups **white bread flour** (see tip)

½ teaspoon **fine sea salt**

DOUGH:

6 tablespoons **water** at about 80°F

3 cups **white bread flour**

1 tablespoon **fine sea salt**

There are two stages involved in making a sourdough: the "sponge"— a reinvigorated starter—and the "dough."

The sponge: In a medium bowl or container that will fit into your refrigerator, combine the water, starter, and white bread flour with a wooden spoon.

It is fine if there are lumps of flour or starter, because as the sponge starts working, it will all meld together. It will have a wonderfully soft and bouncy consistency but be too wet to form a dough at this stage.

Set it aside in a warm area of your kitchen, draped with a clean cloth or plastic wrap. Ideally, the temperature should be in the lower 80's°F. This is easy on a hot summer's day, but in the winter or spring, you might put it near the oven while doing other cooking. Let the sponge rise for 4 hours.

The dough: Put the sponge into a mixing bowl. You can mix by hand, of course, but if you have a freestanding mixer with a dough hook, it will make the job easier. Add all of the dough ingredients and mix for 8–10 minutes. You should end up with a smooth and elastic dough that is just slightly tacky.

If you must knead by hand to feel like you are really making bread, then now is your chance. You really don't need to put flour down on your work surface, so avoid this temptation. Once smooth and elastic, put the dough back in the bowl, cover it again, and place it back in its warm spot for 3–4 hours.

RECIPE CONTINUES ➡

Line a bowl with a piece of cheesecloth or a clean dish towel and generously dust it with flour. Turn out the dough onto your work surface and bang it around a little to knock some of the air out. This also gets the yeasts acting again. Then shape it into a round loaf shape. Put the dough into the flour-lined bowl and cover it with another cloth. Let it sit in the warm spot for about 5 hours.

This is important: Turn your oven on 45 minutes before you are ready to bake. Get it good and hot, as hot as your oven will go. Claire uses an oven thermometer to check that it is at its maximum before proceeding.

Put a baking sheet into the oven to get it really hot, and place another baking sheet, with a rimmed edge (to hold a shallow depth of water) on the floor of your oven. Prepare a pitcher of water next to the oven, ready to pour into the baking sheet. Now, uncover your loaf.

When everything is ready, remove the hot baking sheet from the oven and quickly close the door. It is important to keep the heat in. Now, turn the dough out onto the baking sheet and slice four slits into the top in the shape of a square (or you can develop your own signature cut).

Quickly open the oven, slide the baking sheet in, and pour several tablespoons of water into the rimmed baking sheet on the floor of your oven (be careful the steam does not burn your hand) and slam the door fast.

Set your timer for 20 minutes, and don't peek. Then take a look—the loaf should be golden and sound hollow when tapped. It may need another 15–20 minutes. Claire likes her loaf to get nice and dark, even burned in places. Cool on a wire rack.

=== TIP ===

Organic flour makes a big difference here. The chemicals used to kill pests on the growing wheat will also kill the good organisms needed for the bread to rise properly when using a natural yeast.

GLUTEN-FREE BREAD

MAKES: 1 LOAF
PREP TIME: 20 MINS + RISING · COOK TIME: 55 MINS
WF · GF · V

3¼ cups **gluten-free "brown" bread flour** (available online) or **3 cups gluten-free bread and pizza mix**

½ teaspoon **sea salt**

4½ teaspoons (2 envelopes) **gluten-free instant yeast**

2 tablespoons **honey**

1⅓ cups **milk**

1 tablespoon **apple cider vinegar**

2 tablespoons **olive oil**

2 **eggs**

poppy seeds, to sprinkle

The gluten in a loaf gives it that chewy interior and tender crumb. Take the gluten out and you get something a little denser of crumb and a little more cakelike. In its own right, however, it is satisfying.

Grease an 8½ x 4½ x 2½-inch loaf pan.

Combine the flour, salt, and yeast in a large bowl and set aside.

Warm the honey and milk slightly and remove from the heat. Add the vinegar and oil and whisk in the eggs.

Add the wet ingredients to the dry ingredients and bring together to form a dough. Then shape the dough into a log. Place it in your prepared pan, sprinkle with water, and sprinkle the poppy seeds over the top to cover. Put the dough into a warm place and let rise for 1 hour.

Preheat the oven to 400°F and bake for 45–55 minutes.

Let the loaf cool in the pan for about 5 minutes before turning out onto a wire rack to cool completely.

≡ TIP ≡

Try adding some seeds to the dough to vary the texture and flavor of this loaf. It is always a good idea to soak the seeds overnight before adding them to the bread dough, because soaking the seeds increases the amount of vitamins your body can absorb from them.

BALLYMALOE BROWN SODA BREAD

MAKES: 1 LARGE LOAF OR 2 SMALL LOAVES
PREP TIME: 10 MINS · COOK TIME: 40 MINS
V

2½ cups **whole-wheat flour** (preferably **stone-ground**)

2⅓ cups **all-purpose flour**

2 teaspoons **sea salt**

2 teaspoons **baking soda**, sifted

2⅓ cups **buttermilk**

A traditional version of this yeast-free, cakelike, breakfast bread, created for **Ballymaloe Cookery Course** *by Darina Allen (Kyle, 2001).*

Preheat the oven to 450°F.

Mix all the dry ingredients together in a large, wide bowl, then make a well in the center and pour in all the buttermilk.

Using one hand, stir in a full circle, starting in the center and working toward the outside of the bowl until all the flour is incorporated. The dough should be soft but not too wet and sticky. When it all comes together, in a matter of seconds, turn it out onto a well-floured board.

Wash and dry your hands.

Roll the dough around gently with floury hands for a second, just enough to tidy it up. Flip it over and flatten slightly to about 2 inches.

Sprinkle a little flour onto a baking sheet and place the loaf on top of the flour.

Make a deep X with a knife on top of the loaf and bake in the oven for 15–20 minutes. Reduce the heat to 400°F and bake for another 15–20 minutes, or until the bread sounds hollow when tapped (in some ovens, it may be necessary to turn over the bread 5–10 minutes before the end of baking to cook the other side).

Cool on a wire rack.

TIP

You can add 2 tablespoons oat bran, 1 egg, and 1 tablespoon softened butter to the above recipe to make a richer soda bread dough.

FLATBREAD WITH ZA'ATAR

MAKES: 10
PREP TIME: 30 MINS + RISING · COOK TIME: 10 MINS
DF · V · Ve

2¼ teaspoons (1 envelope) **instant yeast**

⅓ cup warm **water**

3 tablespoons **olive oil**

1⅔ cups **fine farina**

½ cup plus 1 tablespoon **Italian "00" flour** or **all-purpose flour**

1 teaspoon **sea salt**

10 teaspoons **za'atar**

This flatbread actually contains a small amount of yeast, which gives it a little lift. The texture of the dough is dry while you are making it and feels similar to a pasta dough. Both semolina and "00" flour are available in large supermarkets, Italian grocery stores, and gourmet stores. They are worth seeking out for their unique texture.

Dissolve the yeast in the warm water in the bottom of a large mixing bowl. Pour in the olive oil, add the semolina, flour, and salt, and mix it all together coarsely with your hands or a wooden spoon to make a dough.

Cover the bowl and set the dough in a warm place to rise for about 1½ hours.

When the dough has rested, divide it into 10 pieces and roll each piece into a ball. Cover with a clean cloth and let the dough rest again for 10 minutes.

Preheat the oven to 450°F.

Flatten each ball of dough with your hands (1/16 inch thick) and cover with a damp towel for about 30 minutes.

Sprinkle the flatbreads with za'atar and place on baking pans in the oven for about 10 minutes, until crisp and golden. Cool on a wire rack.

≡ TIPS ≡

Za'atar is a flavoring that can be found in large supermarkets, Middle Eastern grocery stores, and some gourmet food stores. If you can't find it, you can make your own by grinding together dried thyme, sesame seeds, and sumac. Cumin, coriander, and nigella seeds also work well.

You can also make the flatbreads without za'atar—sprinkle with a little flaky sea salt once cooked and serve with good-quality green olive oil.

SAVORY
BAKED GOODS

PIZZA DOUGH

MAKES: 2 PIZZAS

PREP TIME: 30 MINS + RISING · COOK TIME: 15 MINS

DF · V · Ve

1 teaspoon **instant yeast**

1¼–1½ cups **water**

4 cups **Italian "00" flour** or
   all-purpose flour, plus extra
   for dusting

olive oil

This is a softer, thicker version of pizza dough than the thin-crust pizzas that are everywhere at the moment. It is super easy to make and super comforting to eat.

In a large bowl, dissolve the yeast in ½ cup of the water. You can use water slightly warm from the faucet to do this, but use cold water for the rest of the dough.

When the yeast has dissolved, add the flour and then up to another ¾ cup water. Mix well to form a soft, pliable dough. Cover and let rest for 10 minutes, then decide at that point whether or not to add the remaining ¼ cup of cold water.

Knead the dough in the bowl until it is smooth and soft. If you want, you can add about ½ cup of sourdough starter (see page 18) to the dough at this stage to give it a delicious sour flavor. Rub a little oil on the dough and cover the bowl with a cloth for 30 minutes.

Once the dough has rested, you will need to add air by kneading it for 5 minutes every 30 minutes. Do this three times.

Now let the dough rise without touching it for 90 minutes in a warmish place in your kitchen.

Preheat the oven to 400°F. Dust 2 baking sheets with flour or line them with parchment paper. Divide the dough into 2 pieces and gently press each piece out into a rectangular shape. Don't roll the dough or you will squeeze the air out of it. Irregularity in the dough is what you are striving for.

Drizzle the dough with olive oil and cover it with the topping of your choice. Bake for about 15 minutes or until golden.

≡ SUGGESTED TOPPINGS ≡

Our favorite topping at the moment is potato & rosemary (see page 34). You will need olive oil, 2 baking potatoes (peeled and sliced $\frac{1}{16}$ inch thick), ¾ cup mascarpone cheese, 1 cup heavy cream, a sprig of fresh rosemary, and salt and pepper to taste. Rub the dough with oil, arrange the potato slices on top, dot with the cheese, and pour over the cream. Sprinkle rosemary leaves over the top and season with salt and pepper.

Other toppings we like:
• Prosciutto, crème fraîche, sage
• Halved cherry tomatoes, salami, mozzarella, finely chopped dried chili
• Sausagemeat, fennel seeds, crème fraîche, blanched broccoli (see page 35)
• Stilton, walnut, endive or other chicory

OAT CRACKERS

MAKES: 12

PREP TIME: 15 MINS + CHILLING · COOK TIME: 12–15 MINS

V

2¾ cups **oat flour**

1⅓ cups **spelt flour**, plus extra for dusting

scant 1 cup **whole-grain spelt flour**

½ teaspoon **baking soda**

2¼ sticks (1 lb 2 oz) **unsalted butter**

1 teaspoon **salt**

1 **egg**

These crackers are buttery and crumbly and the best thing to eat with a hard cheese. They are a Christmas essential with blue cheese.

Mix together the oat flour, spelt flour, and baking soda. Rub the butter into the flour mix between your fingertips until it just about disappears.

Add the salt and egg to bring the dough together, then chill for at least 30 minutes.

Meanwhile preheat the oven to 350°F and line a baking sheet with parchment paper.

Roll out the dough to about ⅛ inch thickness on a lightly floured surface. Cut out the crackers with a round cutter. Alternatively, cut a circle of dough 7 inches in diameter and then cut that into 4 wedges to make 4 large crackers.

Place the crackers on the baking sheet and cook in the oven for 12–15 minutes. They will crisp up as they cool. They can be eaten fresh or stored in a container for up to a week.

≡ TIP ≡

These crackers will absorb moisture and become soft if left out, but they can be recrisped (as can any crackers containing butter) by laying them out on a baking sheet lined with parchment paper and putting them into a preheated oven at 325°F for 5 minutes.

HENRY'S SPICED CHICKEN MYSTERY PIE

SERVES: 4–6

PREP TIME: 10 MINS + COOLING · COOK TIME: 2¾ HOURS

1 large **chicken**

olive oil, for rubbing

6 **rhubarb stalks**, cut into 1-inch pieces

2 **bay leaves**

4 **cardamom pods**, crushed with the
back of a knife

1 glass of **white wine**

2 **onions**, peeled and sliced vertically
into 8 wedges

1 tablespoon **turmeric**

⅔ cup **heavy cream**

1 (12-oz) package **ready-to-bake puff
pastry dough** (or 1 quantity **flaky
dough**, page 212)

1 **egg**, to glaze

salt and freshly ground **black pepper**

*The mystery is that no one can believe it's made with rhubarb. The pink
stalks are wonderful in savory dishes, adding body and a subtle citrus
flavor. Worth trying in lamb stews, too.*

Preheat the oven to 350°F.

Rub the chicken all over with olive oil and plenty of salt and pepper.

Put all the ingredients, except the cream, dough, and egg, into a large casserole dish.
Put the lid on and place in the oven for 1½ –2 hours, until the chicken is falling off the
bone. (Check now and then and add a dash of water if it seems dry.)

Let the chicken stand until cool enough to handle. Pick off the meat and put it into
a pie dish with the vegetables and juice from the casserole, discarding only the skin,
bones, and bay leaves. Stir in the cream and season. You can now put this into the
refrigerator until you want to make the pie (several days later, if you want).

When the filling has cooled completely and you are ready to cook the pie, preheat
the oven to 325°F. Roll out the dough to make the lid, and use the scraps to cut out
a decoration for the top. I like to write the word "Pie." Glaze with the beaten egg.

Cook the pie for 40 minutes or until the top is golden.

FRENCH ONION TART

SPELT DOUGH:

1 cup **white spelt flour**

a pinch of **salt**

a pinch of **sugar**

7 tablespoons cold **unsalted butter**, cut into pieces, plus extra for greasing

¼ cup **iced water**

TOPPING:

3 tablespoons **olive oil**

2 **onions**, thinly sliced

1 teaspoon **vinegar**

small bunch of **thyme**

½ cup **black** or **niçoise olives**

6 **salted anchovy fillets**

1 **egg**, beaten

salt and **black pepper**

═ ALTERNATIVE TOPPINGS ═

• Onions, slices of buffalo mozzarella, and tomato, basil. Drizzle of olive oil.

• Onions, sausage, chopped sage.

• Fine layer of Dijon mustard, onions, slices of tomato, thyme.

• Onions, small pieces of broccoli. Add goat cheese after cooking.

This recipe is an adaptation of the traditional French pissaladière, made with spelt flour. It is simple and the possibilities for toppings are endless.

The spelt dough: Combine the spelt flour, salt, and sugar in a bowl and cut in the butter with a knife. Leave larger chunks of butter than you would think (about the size of a garlic clove) to make the pastry more flaky.

Drizzle in the water and bring it all together in a ball.

Wrap in plastic wrap, and let it rest in the refrigerator for at least 30 minutes.

The topping: Heat the oil in a heavy saucepan and add the sliced onions. Cook the onions for 7–8 minutes, stirring occasionally to be sure they don't burn. You are looking for a caramelized but soft onion.

When cooked, add the vinegar and 2 teaspoons of water. Sprinkle with thyme leaves and transfer into a bowl to cool.

Preheat the oven to 325°F and grease a baking sheet.

Pit and break up the olives a little. On a floured surface, roll out the dough to about ⅛ inch thick and transfer to the baking sheet. Arrange the cooled onions, anchovies, and olives over the dough, leaving a small border, and season with salt and pepper.

Brush the edges with beaten egg, then bake in the oven for 25–30 minutes, until golden and crisp.

ESTHER'S PORK PIE

. . . .

MAKES: 1 LARGE PORK PIE
PREP TIME: 1 HOUR + CHILLING AND COOLING · COOK TIME: 1¾ HOURS

. . . .

3 tablespoons **butter**, diced, plus extra
    for greasing

¼ cup **lard**, diced

⅓ cup **water**

2¼ cups **all-purpose flour**, plus extra
    for dusting

¾ teaspoon **salt**

1 **egg**, beaten, plus extra beaten egg
    for brushing

1 lb 2 oz **pork shoulder** or **leg**

9 oz **pork belly**

9 oz **bacon**

salt, **pepper**, **thyme**, **mace**, **chili**, or
    any other seasoning you want

2½ cups warm **broth**

3 tablespoons **beef gelatin powder**

This recipe is a favorite of Esther Walker, one of Henry's friends.
A traditional British pie that is perfect for picnics.

. . . .

Heat the butter, lard, and water in a saucepan until it is melted and warm, but don't let it boil. While the fat is melting, put the flour and salt into a mixing bowl and make a well in the center. Pour the egg into the well and half mix it in with a knife. When the fat and water have melted together, add to the flour and mix until it forms a dough.

The dough will probably be too sticky, so sprinkle on more flour until it takes on the glossy sheen of dough. Form it into a ball, wrap it in plastic wrap, and chill in the refrigerator for an hour.

When you take it out of the refrigerator, you can cut off one-quarter to put aside for the lid—but I find that if you are using a pie plate (6–6¾ inches in diameter and 6 inches deep), it's easier to roll the whole thing out on a lightly floured surface, lay it over and press it into the greased pie pan, then cut off the excess and reroll that to make the lid.

Don't be afraid to make the walls of the pie really thick—up to about ½ inch. The crust is just a vessel for the pork inside; it will have to be robust enough to contain hot pork fat AND the warm jellied broth you will be pouring in later. If it's a dainty ¼ inch thick, it will tear on cooking.

Preheat your oven to 350°F. Ground the pork and bacon finely in a food processor. Sort through the processed meat to pick out any pieces of gristle or rind.

Add salt, pepper, thyme, mace, chili, or anything else you want to the filling and mix in well. You can test the filling's seasoning by frying a small piece and tasting.

Fill your dough-lined pie plate with the pork filling, really ramming in as much as you can. However much you stuff it, it will all shrink on cooking, so don't be afraid to squash in as much as possible, pummeling it all in, like punching a sleeping bag back into its compression bag.

Now roll out your remaining dough to make the pie lid. You must, must brush beaten egg around the top edges of the pie to seal the lid to the sides. Nothing else will work. If you use anything else, the lid will come away from the sides and the filling will fall out and it will be a disaster.

Lay the lid on top of the pie and press it all around the edges to seal. Trim away the excess dough round the sides.

On the top of the pie, in the center, make a good, generous hole in the dough, about the width of your little finger. This is so that juices can escape during cooking and for pouring in the broth at the end.

Brush the lid with more beaten egg and shove it into the oven for 30 minutes. Then reduce the heat to 325°F and cook for another 1¼ hours.

Let the pie rest in the pie plate to get cool all the way through—this might take 4 or 5 hours. During cooking, the pork will have shrunk away from the sides of the pastry to form a natural cavity to be filled by the gelatin.

RECIPE CONTINUES ⟶

You can make the gelatin in two ways: The first of these is to make up 2½ cups of warm broth—any kind will work, even from a bouillon cube—and set it with gelatin powder. The second, if you're feeling serious, is to ask your butcher for some veal bones or a pig foot. Boil the bones or foot in water for a couple of hours with some carrots and celery and the broth will turn to gelatin when it sets, without needing the help of manufactured gelatin.

Pour the gelatin broth through the hole in the top of the pie while the broth is still lukewarm, and it will set around the pork as it cools. This is not an easy process. You can use a turkey baster if you've got one, or a pitcher and funnel. Don't lose heart if the broth bubbles out of your pie's blowhole and goes everywhere. This kind of pastry is pretty resilient. You may have to repeat the pouring in of the broth after you've poured in the first batch, as it will slowly disappear into the nooks and crannies of the pie and suddenly there will be a ½-inch gap between the lid of the pie and the top of the gelatin. Chill the pie in the refrigerator for at least an hour before eating.

CHEESE EMPANADAS

MAKES: 20 SMALL EMPANADAS
PREP TIME: 30 MINS + RESTING · COOK TIME: 10–15 MINS
V

3¼ cups **all-purpose flour**, plus extra for dusting

2 teaspoons **baking powder**

1 teaspoon **salt**

1 stick (4 oz) **butter**

¼ cup **orange juice**

⅓ cup **sparkling water**

9 oz **mozzarella cheese**

1 **onion**, grated or finely chopped

1½–2 tablespoons **superfine sugar**, plus extra to sprinkle (optional)

1 **egg**, lightly beaten

vegetable oil, for frying (optional)

These are great for parties, because they can be made ahead of time.

Process the flour, baking powder, and salt in a food processor until well mixed.

Add the butter, orange juice, and sparkling water and process until a dough forms.

Transfer the dough onto a surface, bring it together into a ball, wrap it in plastic wrap, and put into the refrigerator for 30 minutes to rest.

Shred the mozzarella into a bowl and add the onion. Add the sugar and mix well.

Preheat the oven to 400°F. Line a baking sheet with parchment paper.

When the dough has rested, remove it from the plastic wrap and dust your work surface with flour. Cut the ball of dough in half (it's easier to roll out smaller amounts). Roll out the dough so that it's about ¹⁄₁₆ inch thick.

Using a 3½–4-inch cutter, cut circles out of the dough. Place a teaspoon of the cheese filling in the center of each circle, fold the dough over to make a half-moon shape, and seal the edges by pressing down with a fork. Make sure they are all well sealed, otherwise the filling will ooze out when you cook them.

Brush the empanadas with the beaten egg, and sprinkle a little sugar over the top of each one if you want that extra sweetness. Place on the baking sheet and cook in the oven for 10–15 minutes, until golden. Cool on a wire rack.

If you want them fried, fill a saucepan 1¼–1½ inch deep with vegetable oil. Heat the oil and deep-fry the empanadas for about 2 minutes on each side or until golden. Sprinkle with superfine sugar before serving.

GLENYS'S DESPERATE DAN STEAK PIE

SERVES: 6

PREP TIME: 20 MINS + COOLING · COOK TIME: 2¾ HOURS

olive oil or vegetable oil

2¾ lb **sirloin steak**, diced

6 **onions**, chopped

8 **bay leaves**

3 ⅓ cups **Newcastle Brown Ale**, or
   a similar sweet ale

sea salt and freshly ground **black pepper**

1 (12-oz) package **ready-to-bake puff
   pastry dough** (or 1 quantity **flaky
   dough**, page 212)

1 **egg**, beaten, for glazing

TO SERVE:

boiled **potatoes** (optional)

wilted **greens** (optional)

≡ TIP ≡

You can make the beef and ale filling
well in advance of assembling it with the
dough, or double up on quantities and
freeze half. Then you need to only defrost
it if you want to make the pie in a hurry.

*Henry's next-door neighbor, Glenys, serves this simple old-fashioned pie
to Andy (her man) when she wants to treat him right.*

Preheat the oven to 325°F.

Heat a dash of oil in a large casserole dish. Add the beef, brown on all sides, and set
aside—you might need to do this in batches to make sure it browns well.

Add a dash more oil to the casserole, add the onions, and cook until golden. Add
the bay leaves and return the meat to the casserole. Add the ale and season well
with salt and pepper.

Cook in the oven for 2 hours, stirring every 45 minutes or so and checking that it
hasn't dried out. You can add more ale, if necessary.

When the meat is tender, let cool and taste for seasoning.

When you are ready to assemble the pie, preheat the oven to 325°F. Transfer the
cooled meat mixture to a pie plate and top with the rolled puff pastry dough. Press
the dough around the rim to seal. If you are feeling creative, try making shapes from
the leftover scraps of dough. The children can help.

Glaze the top of the dough with the beaten egg, using a pastry brush, and make
a hole in the middle to let steam escape. Bake for 40 minutes, or until the pastry
is golden and you can see the juices bubbling up. Serve with boiled potatoes and
wilted greens.

SALMON & DILL MUFFINS

MAKES: 6
PREP TIME: 15 MINS · COOK TIME: 20 MINS

2 cups **all-purpose flour**

2 teaspoons **baking powder**

1½ cups **shredded cheese**

1¾ oz **smoked salmon**, chopped

⅓ cup chopped **fresh dill**

1 **egg**

¾ cup **buttermilk**

5 tablespoons **vegetable** or **sunflower oil**

⅓ cup **cream cheese**

A breakfast muffin that isn't sweet.

Preheat the oven to 350°F and line a 6-cup muffin pan with paper liners.

Mix the flour and baking powder together in a large bowl. Add the shredded cheese, smoked salmon, and dill.

In a separate bowl, beat together the egg, buttermilk, and oil.

Place half the wet ingredients into the dry ingredients and stir well. Then add the rest of the wet ingredients and mix until completely combined.

Spoon into the muffin liners until each is filled halfway, then place a heaping teaspoon of cream cheese in the middle of each muffin. Top them off until they are full with the muffin batter.

Cook for 10 minutes, then take the pan out and turn it around so the muffins cook evenly. Put the pan back into the oven and continue to cook for another 10 minutes or until the muffins are just browning on top.

SWEET PIES & PASTRIES

LEON PECAN PIE

SERVES: 8–10

PREP TIME: 30 MINS + CHILLING · COOK TIME: 1 HOUR 10 MINS

WF · GF · V

1¼ sticks (5 oz) **butter**, plus extra
for greasing

½ cup **superfine sugar**

1 **egg**, plus 1 **yolk**

1⅔ cups **gluten-free all-purpose flour**,
plus extra for dusting

FILLING:

3½ tablespoons **butter**

1 cup **golden syrup** or **dark corn syrup**

2 tablespoons **superfine sugar**

1 teaspoon **cornstarch**

2 extra-large **eggs**

2 cups **pecan halves**

A simple, rich, gluten-free pecan tart that was a staple in our restaurant for years. Baked by Craig Barton, one of our favorite bakers.

For the dough, cream together the butter and sugar with a wooden spoon or in a freestanding electric mixer until smooth.

Add the egg and egg yolk and mix until completely incorporated. Add the flour and quickly bring it together in a ball. Wrap the dough tightly in plastic wrap and refrigerate for at least 30 minutes.

Grease a 9–10-inch fluted tart pan. Roll out the dough on a floured surface to about ⅛ inch thick and line your tart pan with it. Trim the edges and chill in the refrigerator for 30 minutes. Meanwhile, preheat the oven to 325°F.

Line the chilled pastry shell with parchment paper, and fill it with pie weights to stop it from shrinking while it's being baked. Bake in the oven for 20 minutes, then remove the weights and paper. Return to the oven and bake for another 5 minutes. The pastry should be a nice blonde color. Set aside to cool.

Put the butter and golden syrup or corn syrup into a medium saucepan over low heat. When it becomes liquid, remove it from the heat and whisk in the sugar. Let cool a little.

In a small bowl, whisk the cornstarch and eggs until smooth and add to the saucepan.

Fill the baked pastry with the pecan halves. Pour the golden syrup mixture on top and fill it up to just below the edge of the shell. Put into the oven, being careful to avoid spilling any liquid over the sides, because this might make it difficult to remove it from the pan once it's baked.

Bake for about 40 minutes, or until the tart is a dark golden color and has slightly risen in the middle. Remove from the oven and let cool in the pan.

TIP

This can be served cold for tea, or warm with ice cream.

PHOTOGRAPH ON PAGES 56–57 ➜

DITTISHAM PLUM CRISP

2¼ lb tart **plums**

¼ cup **superfine sugar**

3 tablespoons **gluten-free all-purpose flour**

1 tablespoon **sweet white wine**

CRUMB TOPPING:

⅔ cup **gluten-free all-purpose flour**

1 cup **almond meal**

½ cup **slivered almonds**

⅓ cup packed **light brown sugar**

a pinch of **sea salt**

¼ teaspoon **ground cinnamon**

1¼ sticks (5 oz) cold **unsalted butter**, cut into ½-inch cubes

Crisps (known as crumbles in the UK) are all about getting the balance right between sweet and sour and soft and crisp. This makes a wonderful conclusion to a simple summer meal.

Preheat the oven to 350°F.

Halve and pit the plums and put into a bowl. Toss with the sugar, flour, and wine and put into a deep 9–10-inch baking dish.

Put all the crumb topping ingredients into a bowl and use the back of a fork or two knives to break up the chunks of butter into tiny pieces.

Sprinkle the topping lightly over the fruit and place in the oven.

Bake for 40–45 minutes, or until the fruit is bubbling and the topping is golden.

TIP

Almonds and plums go together well, but you can substitute them hazelnuts and blueberries, or walnuts and apples.

KEY LIME PIE

SERVES: 6–8

PREP TIME: 20 MINS · COOK TIME: 25–35 MINS

V

1¾ cups **graham crackers** crumbs

6 tablespoons **unsalted butter**, melted

1 (14-oz) can **sweetened condensed milk**

4 extra-large **egg yolks**

1 tablespoon **lime zest**, plus extra for garnish (about 3 limes)

½ cup freshly squeezed **lime juice**

1½ cups **heavy cream**, chilled

Key limes come from the Florida Keys (hence the name) and tend to be smaller and sweeter than conventional limes. If you can't get to Florida for your groceries, don't worry—the flavor will still be wonderful.

Preheat the oven to 350°F.

Combine the graham cracker crumbs and melted butter in a medium bowl and mix well. Press the mixture into a 9-inch pie pan and bake in the oven until lightly browned. This will take 12–15 minutes. Remove from the oven and transfer the pie pan to a wire rack until completely cooled.

Reduce the oven temperature to 325°F.

In a medium bowl, gently whisk together the condensed milk, egg yolks, and lime zest and juice. Pour into the prepared, cooled crust.

Return the pie to the oven and bake until the center is set but still quivers when the pan is nudged. This should take 15–20 minutes.

Let the pie cool completely in the pan on top of a wire rack.

Once the pie has cooled, put it into the refrigerator to chill until ready to serve.

Before serving, lightly whip the cream into soft peaks. Spread the cream over the chilled pie. Garnish with a little more lime zest.

TIP

To crush the cookie crumbs, simply put the graham crackers (or you could substitute them with gingersnaps) into a thick plastic bag and smash them with a rolling pin.

STRAWBERRY & BLUEBERRY COBBLER

SERVES: 6

PREP TIME: 15 MINS + RESTING · COOK TIME: 40 MINS

WF · GF · V

1¾ cup **blueberries**

3¼ cups hulled and quartered **strawberries**

¼ cup **superfine sugar**

¼ cup **cornstarch**

1¼ cups **gluten-free all-purpose flour**

1 tablespoon **gluten-free baking powder**

a large pinch of **salt**

3½ **unsalted butter**, cut into small cubes

⅔ cup **heavy cream**, plus extra for brushing

Cobblers are the perfect summer dessert. (In fact, they make a damned good summer Sunday breakfast.) The cobbler topping is like an American biscuit or British scone and melts into the jammy fruit. Serve this one with thick cream.

Preheat the oven to 350°F.

Combine the berries, sugar, and cornstarch and put the mix into a deep 1–1½-quart baking dish.

Put the flour, baking powder, salt, and butter into a bowl and use the back of a fork or two knives to break up the chunks of butter into tiny pieces. Pour over the cream and mix until it all comes together.

Press the topping into a ball and place on a floured work surface. Let the mixture rest for 10 minutes. Then roll out the dough to a ¾ inch thickness and cut out circles with a cookie cutter.

Lay the circles flat over the fruit, brush with extra cream, and place on a baking pan to catch any drips.

Bake in the oven for 35–40 minutes, or until the fruit is bubbling and the topping is golden brown.

≡ TIPS ≡

You can also make this cobbler topping with regular all-purpose flour.

Try experimenting with different fruits. Peaches and nectarines work well, with a little added lemon zest and juice.

HATTIE'S BLACK CURRANT TART CANELLE

SERVES: 6–8

PREP TIME: 25 MINS + CHILLING · COOK TIME: 25 MINS

V

1⅓ cups **all-purpose flour**, plus extra
for dusting

6 tablespoons **unsalted butter**, plus
extra for greasing

⅓ cup **superfine sugar**, plus extra
for sprinkling

2 **egg yolks**

1 tablespoon **water**

1 tablespoon **ground cinnamon**

vanilla ice cream or **crème fraîche**,
to serve

FILLING:

2 cups **black currants** or blueberries

extra **superfine sugar** to add to
the berries

milk or **beaten egg**, to glaze

Preheat the oven to 350°F and grease a 7-inch fluted tart pan.

To make the dough in a food processor, add the flour, butter, sugar, egg yolks, water, and cinnamon and process until it comes together into a ball. Remove from the machine, cover with plastic wrap, and chill well for at least an hour in the refrigerator.

To make the dough by hand, rub together the flour, butter, sugar, and cinnamon with your fingers until you have a bread crumblike consistency. Slowly add the egg yolks and water until the mixture comes together into a ball. Cover with plastic wrap and chill well.

Put the black currants or blueberries into a saucepan, cover generously with superfine sugar, and put over low heat. Stir regularly, and when you are sure that all the sugar has dissolved, turn up the heat until the fruit is bubbling and thickened. Remove from the heat.

Roll out the dough on a floured surface to ½ inch thick and line the tart pan, gathering up any scraps. Fill the tart shell with the fruit compote, and roll out the scraps to make an extra thin strip to go around the edge for a tidy finish. There should be enough leftover dough to make a lattice pattern over the top of the tart, if you want.

Brush the pastry with milk or beaten egg, and bake in the oven for 20–25 minutes, until the pastry is golden. Serve cool, with vanilla ice cream or crème fraîche.

MAGGIE'S CROATIAN PEAR PIE

¾ cup plus 2 tablespoons **superfine sugar** or ¾ cup packed **light brown sugar**

1 stick (4 oz) **unsalted butter**, plus extra for greasing

3 cups **all-purpose flour**, plus extra for dusting

1 **egg**

¼ teaspoon **baking powder**

a pinch of **salt**

4–6 ripe **pears**

⅓ cup **apricot preserves**

cream or **vanilla ice cream**, to serve (optional)

ALMOND FILLING:

1¾ sticks (7 oz) **unsalted butter**, softened

1⅔ cups **confectioners' sugar**

2 **eggs**, plus 2 **yolks**

a dash of **apple brandy** (optional), or other alcohol

1 cup **almond meal**

½ cup **all-purpose flour**

This pie can be done in a square, oval, loaf, or any shape pan you want. Also, the pears can be cut into halves, quarters, or slices, depending on the look you like.

Preheat the oven to 425°F and grease a 10-inch tart pan.

To make the dough, beat together the sugar and butter until you get a smooth paste. Add the flour, egg, baking powder, and salt and mix well, adding a little water if you need to. The dough will be crumbly, but do not worry—it's supposed to be like that.

Roll out the dough on a floured surface and line the tart pan, pricking it all over with a fork. If the dough is too crumbly, press it into the pan by hand a little at a time. Theh pie should have a thick crust of pastry, so don't be alarmed by the amount you have. Line it with parchment paper and fill with pie weights. Bake for 8–10 minutes, depending on your oven, then remove the paper and weights and let cool.

Reduce the oven temperature to 350°F.

Peel the pears, leaving the stems on. Cut them into slices or halve them, removing the core carefully so they don't break.

To make the almond filling, cream together the butter and sugar, then add the eggs and egg yolks one at a time, mixing after each addition. You can do this by hand or using an electric handheld mixer. Add the alcohol, if you are using it, then the almond meal and flour, and mix well.

Pour the filling into the pastry shell, and arrange the pears on top any way you want.

Bake the pie in the oven for 30–40 minutes, or until golden brown, but do not let it burn. Let cool in the pan.

Heat the apricot preserves in a small saucepan with a teaspoon or two of water until it is runny and spreadable, and while still warm, use a pastry brush to glaze your pie. Eat this pie lukewarm on its own, with cream or a good vanilla ice cream.

TIP

If you are making this in a loaf pan, bake for another 20 minutes on a low oven shelf.

PHOTOGRAPH ON PAGES 68–69 ⟶

APPLE CRISP

SERVES: 6

PREP TIME: 20 MINS · COOK TIME: 35 MINS

V (GF if gluten-free bread is used)

3¼ lb **apples**, peeled, quartered, and cored

juice of 1 **lemon**

⅓ cup **superfine sugar**, plus an extra 2 tablespoons for sprinkling

¼ teaspoon **ground cinnamon**

7 slices stale, **crusty white bread**, crusts removed, torn into pieces

7 tablespoons **salted butter**, melted

light cream, to serve

A very easy dessert, and a great way to turn your stale bread into something delicious and sumptuous.

Preheat the oven to 350°F.

Combine the apples, lemon juice, sugar, and cinnamon and put into a deep 1–1½-quart baking dish.

In a bowl, toss the bread pieces in the melted butter and then arrange in a layer over the apples. Sprinkle sugar over the top and place on a baking pan to catch any drips.

Bake in the oven for 30–35 minutes, or until the fruit is bubbling and the topping is golden. Serve hot with light cream.

TIPS

Try using pears instead of apples and add a splash of white wine.

Don't use sourdough or levain bread, because it will be too sour. Use plain white bread or a French stick or baguette, nice and stale.

JANET'S LONDON FIELDS
APRICOT & CHERRY GALETTE

SERVES 6–8
PREP TIME: 30 MINS + CHILLING · COOK TIME: 45–50 MINS
V

2 tablespoons **sugar**

1 tablespoon **all-purpose flour**

1 tablespoon **almond meal** (optional)

1 lb fresh **apricots**, washed, halved , and pitted

1⅔ cups **cherries**, washed and pitted

1 **egg**, beaten

vanilla ice cream or **whipped cream**, to serve (optional)

DOUGH:

1 cup **all-purpose flour**, plus extra for dusting

a pinch of **salt**

a pinch of **sugar**

6 tablespoons cold **unsalted butter**, cut into ½-inch pieces

¼ cup **ice-cold water**

= TIP =

This is basically a free-form, open-face tart and it can be used for all different kinds of fruit.

For the dough, combine the flour, salt, and sugar in a bowl and either cut in the cold butter with the back of a fork or use two knives.

Avoid overmixing—leaving larger chunks of butter than you would expect will make the pastry more flaky. Drizzle in the water and bring it all together into a ball without working the dough. Wrap in plastic wrap, then flatten into a disk and let it rest in the refrigerator for about 45 minutes.

Preheat the oven to 400°F and line a baking pan with parchment paper. Let the dough to come to room temperature so it's easier to work.

Dust a work surface with flour and roll out the dough into a circle about the size of a dinner plate. Put it into the baking pan and refrigerate for a few minutes.

Remove the dough circle from the refrigerator and sprinkle the sugar, flour, and almond meal over it, leaving a 1–1¼-inch border around the outside. Arrange the fruit on top of the almonds—you can put the cherries in the middle and the apricots in a circle around them, or make up your own pattern.

Fold over the dough rim to create a crust. Brush the rim with beaten egg, and bake in the bottom half of the oven for 45–50 minutes, until the fruit is squashy.

When cooked, transfer the galette to a wire rack to cool.

Serve warm or cold, with vanilla ice cream or whipped cream. Or simply enjoy it on its own with a warm beverage.

ANDI'S MARSHMALLOW-TOPPED SWEET POTATO PIE

SERVES: 6–8

PREP TIME: 25 MINS · COOK TIME: 50 MINS

V

flour, for dusting

butter, for greasing

1 (12-oz) package **pie dough**

4 **pink-fleshed sweet potatoes**

6 tablespoons of **honey**, **agave nectar**
  or any sweetener that you prefer

1 teaspoon **ground nutmeg**

1 teaspoon **ground cinnamon**

1 teaspoon **ground allspice**

1 teaspoon **vanilla extract**

2 tablespoons **dried unsweetend**
  coconut flakes (optional)

3 **egg whites**

1 package **white mini marshmallows**

Preheat the oven to 350°F and grease a 10–11-inch fluted tart pan.

Roll out the dough on a floured work surface and use to line the tart pan. Line the pastry shell with parchment paper, and fill it with pie weights to stop it from shrinking while it's being baked. Bake in the oven for 25 minutes, until the pastry is golden, then remove from the oven, take out the paper and weights, and set aside to cool, leaving the oven on.

Meanwhile, peel the sweet potatoes and cut them into cubes. Boil until soft, then drain and mash them well.

Put the sweet potatoes into a large bowl with the honey, nutmeg, cinnamon, allspice, vanilla extract, and coconut (if using). Mix thoroughly.

Beat the egg whites well in a separate bowl, then add to the sweet potatoes and whip the mixture together for a few minutes. Pour into the pastry shell and bake in the oven for about 20 minutes, until the top of the pie has a few browned peaks.

Gently arrange the marshmallows on top in any design that you like.

When you are ready to eat the pie, place it under a hot broiler to toast the marshmallows, which will turn golden and start to melt quickly. Keep a close eye on it so they don't burn. Serve immediately.

PUMPKIN PIE

SERVES: 8–10

PREP TIME: 25 MINS · COOK TIME: 35 MINS

V

2 cups store-bought **pumpkin puree** (or homemade—see tip)

3 **eggs**

scant ½ cup **heavy cream**

⅔ cup packed **light brown sugar**

1 teaspoon **ground cinnamon**

½ teaspoon **ground ginger**

½ teaspoon **ground star anise**

½ teaspoon **ground allspice**

1 teaspoon **sea salt**

3 tablespoons **maple syrup**

finely grated **fresh ginger** (optional)

black pepper (optional)

1 quantity **basic pie dough** (see page 212) or 1 (9-inch) **ready-to-bake pie crust**

flour, for dusting

butter, for greasing

Chantilly cream, to serve

A warm, deeply spicy version of this traditional Thanksgiving treat.

Preheat the oven to 350°F and grease a 9-inch fluted tart pan with a loose bottom.

Whisk all the ingredients together, except the ginger, black pepper, and dough, in a large bowl. The pie will be silkier if the pumpkin is as smooth as possible, so push the filling through a fine strainer.

Taste the filling. At this point, you can add a little finely grated fresh ginger, along with a good grinding of black pepper to taste, if you want.

Roll out the dough on a lightly floured surface as thinly as possible and press into the tart pan, then trim the edges. Pour the filling into the pastry shell and bake in the oven for about 35 minutes, or until the custardy filling is just set while retaining a slight wobble.

Cool and serve with penty of Chantilly cream (heavy cream sweetened with superfine sugar and a dash of vanilla extract).

☰ TIP ☰

To make your own puree, cut a butternut squash in half, remove the seeds, and bake it in a hot oven, cut side down. When soft, scrape out the flesh and puree. You can also do this with a small pumpkin, but you might need to add butternut squash puree to sweeten it.

CLAIRE'S CHERRY PIE

SERVES 8

PREP TIME: 40 MINS · COOK TIME: 1 HOUR

V

butter, for greasing

1⅙ quantity **basic pie dough**
   (see page 212)

3¼ cups fresh or frozen pitted
   sour cherries

1 cup **superfine sugar**

¼ cup **cornstarch**

a pinch of **salt**

1 **egg**

a little **milk**

Sour cherries are a favorite as a pie filling. Cherries are best when freshly picked off the trees in spring or summer. If you can't find fresh cherries, you can use frozen or canned ones.

Preheat the oven to 400°F and grease an 8–9-inch pie plate or fluted tart pan.

Roll out half of the dough into a disk large enough to line the pie plate with some excess. Place the disk of dough in the dish, pressing down well. Roll the other half of the dough into a rectangle ⅟₁₆ inch thick and place it on a baking sheet lined with parchment paper. Place both in the refrigerator while you prepare the filling.

Put the cherries, sugar, and cornstarch into a bowl and add the salt. Toss to coat the fruit evenly.

Remove the pie plate from the refrigerator and fill it with the cherry mixture. Remove the rectangle of dough from the refrigerator and use a small knife to slice the dough into ¾-inch strips. Arrange the strips of dough over the cherries in a lattice pattern.

Crack the egg into a small bowl and add a few drops of milk. Whisk to combine. Trim the edges of the dough to the rim of the dish. Using a pastry brush, carefully coat the lattice with egg wash.

Place the pie in the oven for about an hour, with a piece of aluminum foil underneath to catch any drips. The pie is ready when you see the fruit filling bubbling through.

TARTE TATIN

1 (9-oz) sheet store-bought **puff pastry**
flour, for dusting
4–6 medium **apples** (Pippin and Granny
Smiths are good)
juice of ½ **lemon**
2 tablespoons **unsalted butter**
⅓ cup **superfine sugar**
single cream, to serve

Crisp pastry and warm, soft caramelized apples in a pool of cream.

Preheat the oven to 400°F. Line a baking sheet with parchment paper.

On a lightly floured surface, roll the dough into a 12-inch disk. Use a sharp knife to carefully trim the edge, making as perfect a disk as you can without losing too much of the diameter. Place the dough circle carefully on the lined baking sheet. Place it in the freezer if it will fit; if not, place it in the refrigerator.

Peel, quarter, and core the apples, then coat in the lemon juice.

Place a 10–12-inch tatin dish or a medium ovenproof skillet on medium heat and melt the butter until it foams. Add the sugar and let it dissolve. Increase the heat and continue to cook until the sugar just starts to caramelize (turns light brown). Remove from the heat. The caramel will continue to darken as it cools, so take it off the heat well before it reaches a dark caramel.

Arrange the apples tightly in the pan in 2 layers.

Place the chilled circle of dough over the top of the pan and tuck the edges down inside. Pierce the dough with a knife to let steam escape during baking.

Place the pan in the oven and bake for about 30 minutes, until the pastry is golden and the juices are bubbling. Remove from the oven and let rest for 5 minutes.

Run a small knife around the edge of the pan to release the tart. Place a serving plate slightly larger than the tart pan over the tart, and carefully flip the tart over onto the plate. Drizzle any juices over the tart then serve hot with plenty of light cream.

≡ TIPS ≡

If you are unsure about when to stop cooking the caramel, you can make it as dark as you like it and then stop the cooking process by dunking the bottom of the pan in a sink full of ice-cold water. This will arrest the cooking so that the caramel does not burn.

Try swapping the apples for pears or quinces.

CAKES

SIMNEL CAKE

SERVES: 10–12

PREP TIME: 1 HOUR · COOK TIME: 3½ HOURS

V

1¾ cups **all-purpose flour**

½ teaspoon **salt**

¼ teaspoon freshly grated **nutmeg**

½ teaspoon **ground cinnamon**

¼ teaspoon **allspice**

1½ sticks (6 oz) **unsalted butter**, plus extra for greasing

¾ cup packed **Demerara sugar** or **light brown sugar**

2 tablespoons **dark treacle** or **molasses**

3 **eggs**, plus extra to glaze

3 cups **dried currants**

2 cups **golden raisins**

¾ cup good-quality **candied peel**

zest and juice of 1 **lemon**

½ cup **almond meal**

⅔ cup **whole milk**

a little **apricot preserves**

MARZIPAN:

3⅔ cups **confectioners' sugar**

4¾ cups **almond meal**

2 **eggs**

1 teaspoon **lemon juice**

1 teaspoon **almond extract**

This recipe is from Petra, Henry's mother-in-law. Simnel cake is a British Easter tradition. It is widely accepted that the balls of marzipan on top are meant to represent the disciples, but there is some debate on how many there should be: 11 if you exclude the traitor Judas, 12 if you count him in, or 13 to include Jesus. Petra's homemade marzipan is so good that we recommend 13—every time you leave the room, you will return to find that another ball has mysteriously vanished.

First make the marzipan. Sift the confectioners' sugar into a bowl, then add the almond meal, eggs, lemon juice, and almond extract to taste—add the extract slowly and keep tasting, because some brands are stronger than others. Form into a ball and knead lightly. Divide into 3 pieces and wrap each one tightly in plastic wrap until ready to use.

Preheat the oven to 300°F. Line a deep 8-inch cake pan with parchment paper.

Sift the flour, salt, and spices together and set aside.

In another bowl, cream the butter, sugar, and black treacle or molasses until light and fluffy. Add the eggs one at a time, sprinkling in a little of the sifted flour and beating well after each addition. Stir in the remaining flour, then the fruit, peel, zest, juice, and almond meal. Add the milk and mix until all the ingredients are well combined.

Roll out one of the pieces of marzipan into an 8-inch disk. Turn half the cake batter into the pan, level it out and cover it with this disk of marzipan. Then cover with the rest of the cake batter and smooth the top.

Bake in the oven for about 3½ hours, or until a toothpick inserted into the center of the cake comes out clean. The top of the cake should be dull, not shiny.

When the cake is completely cooled, brush the top with a little warmed preserves, strained if necessary. Roll out another ball of marzipan and place it on top of the cake, pressing it down well. Score the top in a crosshatch pattern. Brush with a little lightly beaten egg.

Turn the broiler or oven to high. Divide the remaining ball of marzipan into 11, 12, or 13 balls, as you prefer, and arrange them around the edge of the cake. Brush each ball with egg and put the cake into the oven or under the broiler for a few minutes to give it an attractive, toasted appearance.

═ TIPS ═

Petra says the downfall of Simnel cake is twiggy currants. She always picks them over to remove the little twigs.

If your oven tends to be hot, wrap a second layer of paper around the outside of the cake pan to keep it from getting too dark.

If you are serving the cake to the young, elderly, or infirm, try use pasteurized eggs—or eggs from flocks you trust— for making the marzipan.

PHOTOGRAPH ON PAGES 86–87 ➜

LIFE BY CHOCOLATE CAKE

SERVES: 10–12
PREP TIME: 20 MINS · COOK TIME: 45–50 MINS
WF · GF · V

5 **eggs**

1 cup packed **light brown sugar**

scant ½ cup **instant espresso**

12 oz **semisweet chocolate**, broken into pieces

2¼ sticks (9 oz) **unsalted butter**, cut into small pieces

1 teaspoon **vanilla extract**

a pinch of **sea salt**

This flourless chocolate cake is SO rich, yet superlight, like a mousse. After you have made it once, you will make it again and again, not least because your friends and family will give you no choice. You have been warned.

Preheat the oven to 325°F. Line a 9-inch cake pan, preferably not one with a loose bottom, with parchment paper.

With an electric handheld mixer, beat the eggs and ½ cup of the sugar until the mixture forms voluminous peaks.

In a saucepan, dissolve the remaining sugar in the coffee over medium heat, then stir in the chocolate pieces and butter and remove from the heat.

Add the vanilla and salt to the saucepan and stir occasionally until everything is completely melted.

In a steady stream, pour the melted chocolate mixture into the whisked eggs and stir just until combined.

Pour into the prepared cake pan, then place in a deep roasting pan and pour enough hot water into the roasting pan to reach almost to the top of the cake pan.

Bake in the oven for 45–50 minutes. The cake should be set but not solid. Let cool in the pan.

TIP

This cake tastes even more beautiful with a little dollop of crème fraîche.

CLEMENTINE CORNMEAL CAKE

SERVES: 12

PREP TIME: 25 MINS + COOLING · COOK TIME: 50 MINS

WF · GF · V

2¼ sticks (9 oz) **unsalted butter**, softened, plus extra for greasing

1¼ cups **superfine sugar**

2 **eggs**

1½ cups **cornmeal**

1 cup **almond meal**

1 teaspoon **gluten-free baking powder**

zest and juice of 3 **clementines**

2 tablespoons **lemon juice**

Greek yogurt or **heavy cream**, to serve

SYRUP:

¼ cup **golden honey**

juice of 1 **clementine** and 1 **lemon**

This moist flourless cake is perfect for an afternoon snack, but it also makes a beautiful afterdinner dessert when drizzled with a little cream or topped with a blob of yogurt.

Preheat the oven to 340°F. Line a 10-inch round cake pan with parchment paper.

In a large mixing bowl, beat the soft butter and sugar until pale and fluffy. Add the eggs one at a time, beating well after each addition.

In a separate bowl, whisk together by hand the cornmeal, almond meal, and baking powder. Add to the butter mixture and beat well. Fold in the clementine zest and juice and lemon juice before scraping the batter into the prepared pan.

Bake in the oven for 50 minutes, or until a toothpick inserted into the center of the cake comes out clean.

To make the syrup, heat the honey with the clementine and lemon juice in a small saucepan over low heat until runny, then pour over the cake while it's still hot. Let cool in the pan. Serve with Greek yogurt or heavy cream.

≡ TIP ≡

You can experiment with other kinds of citrus in this recipe as well. It works well with lemon. You can use agave nectar instead of honey for the syrup (it would also go well with lime juice in place of the clementines).

PINEAPPLE UPSIDE-DOWN CAKE

SERVES: 6

PREP TIME: 25 MINS + RESTING · COOK TIME: 45 MINS

V

1 stick (4 oz) **unsalted butter**, softened

scant 1 cup **superfine sugar**

2 **eggs**

1 teaspoon **vanilla extract**

1 teaspoon **salt**

scant ½ cup **whole milk**

1⅔ cups **all-purpose flour**

2 teaspoons **baking powder**

½ **pineapple**, skin and core removed,
cut into rings (or canned pineapple,
if you prefer)

CARAMEL:

1 stick (4 oz) **unsalted butter**

¾ cup packed **light brown sugar**

≡ TIP ≡

If the cake sticks, you can either
put it back into the oven to melt
the caramel a little, or place the pan
directly on the heat of the stove
for a minute (no longer, or it could
burn), which will melt the caramel
and help release the cake.

*A carnival cake. Full of life. Full of flavor. A little kitsch. But deeply
satisfying. You can easily substitute the flour with white spelt flour.*

Preheat the oven to 340°F.

First make the caramel. Put the butter and brown sugar into the bottom of a deep
8-inch cake pan and place the pan directly over low heat on the stove. Stir constantly
until the butter-sugar mixture comes together and bubbles. Set aside to cool.

Cream the butter and superfine sugar until light and fluffy. Add the eggs one at
a time and mix until incorporated. Add the vanilla and salt. Add half the milk and mix.

Sift together the flour and baking powder and add half to the mixture. Add the
remaining milk and finally the rest of the flour.

Now that the caramel in the pan has cooled, cover it with the pineapple rings. Over
that, pour the cake batter and smooth the surface. Bake in the oven for about
40 minutes, until the top of the cake springs back when lightly pressed with a finger.

Let the cake sit in the pan for about 15 minutes before running a knife around the
edge and inverting it onto a serving plate. If it is too hot, it can fall apart.

TOMMI'S MORE-THAN-FRUIT CAKE

SERVES: 8
PREP TIME: 25 MINS + COOLING • COOK TIME: 55–60 MINS
V

scant 1⅔ cups **red wine**

2 cups chopped **dried figs**

1½ teaspoons **ground cinnamon**

¼ teaspoon **ground cloves**

1 stick (4 oz) **unsalted butter**, cold

¾ cup **honey**, plus extra for drizzling

1 **egg**, lightly beaten

1¾ cups **spelt flour**

1½ teaspoons **baking powder**

1 teaspoon **baking soda**

Greek yogurt or **sour cream**, to serve

Red wine and figs have a special affinity for one another and the spices in this recipe. The fig seeds create a wonderful popping sensation as they burst in your mouth. Also a great way to use up leftover red wine.

Preheat the oven to 325°F. Line an 8-inch square cake pan with parchment paper.

Put the red wine, figs, and spices into a medium saucepan and bring to a boil.

When the fruit has plumped up a little (about 5 minutes), remove the saucepan from the heat and let o cool for 10 minutes. Stir in the butter and honey and let stand for another 10 minutes. Stir in the egg.

Sift the flour, baking powder, and baking soda into a large mixing bowl. Pour the fig mixture over the flour mixture and stir just until mixed. Pour into the prepared pan.

Bake for 55–60 minutes, or until a toothpick inserted into the center of the cake comes out clean. Let cool in the pan. Serve with Greek yogurt or sour cream, with extra honey for drizzling.

TIP

Can be served as an afterdinner dessert or as an afternoon snack. A chunk in the lunch bag also makes a great midmorning snack.

HANNAH'S BANANA BREAD

SERVES: 8–10

PREP TIME: 25 MINS + COOLING · COOK TIME: 55 MINS–1 HOUR

V

½ cup **pecan halves**

⅔ cup **vegetable oil**, plus extra for greasing

1 cup packed **dark brown sugar**

1 teaspoon **vanilla extract**

2 **eggs**

3 ripe **bananas**, peeled

⅓ cup **plain yogurt**

1 teaspoon **baking soda**

1 teaspoon **baking powder**

½ teaspoon **ground cinnamon**

¼ teaspoon **salt**

2 cups **whole-grain spelt flour**

TOPPING:

1 **banana**, peeled

3 tablespoons **superfine sugar**

Some time ago people started leaving wishes on pieces of paper in a drawer in the Ludgate Circus branch of Leon. Hannah's wish was to have a cake named after her. Hence the name. This version of the traditional bread is made with spelt flour and a banana that sinks into the bread during cooking. It is the best banana bread we have tasted.

Preheat the oven to 340°F. Line a 9 x 5 x 3-inch loaf pan with parchment paper. Line a baking sheet with parchment paper as well.

Spread out the pecans over the lined baking sheet and toast them in the oven for 5–7 minutes, or until lightly golden and fragrant. Set aside to cool.

In a large bowl, whisk together the oil, dark brown sugar, vanilla, and eggs.

In a separate bowl, set aside a banana and coarsely mash the remaining bananas. Add the yogurt and mix well. Sift the baking soda, baking powder, and cinnamon over the yogurt mixture, add the salt, and stir well to combine.

Now add the banana mixture to the egg mixture and stir to combine. Chop the pecans into small pieces and add them with the flour, stirring just until incorporated. Spoon the batter into the prepared loaf pan.

Carefully slice the reserved banana in half lengthwise. Place one half, cut side up, on top of the bread and sprinkle with the superfine sugar. (Eat the other half.)

Bake in the oven for 55–60 minutes, or until the bread is springy to the touch and a toothpick inserted into the center of the cake comes out clean. Cool in the pan for at least 10 minutes before turning it out onto a wire rack to cool.

TIP

Never overmix the batter for quick breads like this, because they can easily turn tough and rubbery.

VANILLA CUPCAKES

MAKES: 12 CUPCAKES
PREP TIME: 15 MINS · COOK TIME: 25 MINS
WF · GF · DF · V · Ve

1¾ cups **gluten-free all-purpose flour**

⅔ cup **potato flour** or **cornstarch**

⅔ cup **coconut flour**

1¾ teaspoons **baking powder**

1 tablespoon **flax meal** (optional)

1½ teaspoons **sea salt**

⅔ cup **coconut oil**, melted

1 cup **agave nectar**

2 tablespoons **vanilla extract**

⅔ cup **rice milk**

½ teaspoon **baking soda**

scant ½ cup boiling **water**

≡ TIPS ≡

You can omit the flax meal if you don't have it on hand, but it adds nutrition, texture, and a nutty quality. To make your own, grind up some flaxseed.

The coconut oil can be replaced with a good-quality tasteless oil, such as sunflower, but only if you really must. Coconut oil is full of nutrition.

These are delicious iced with the Vegan Vanilla Frosting (see page 101).

These cupcakes are free from wheat, refined sugar, dairy, and egg. But, miraculously, they are still full of flavor and indulgence. If you don't like the flavor of coconut, 1. you're crazy and 2. you can replace the coconut flour with almond meal.

Preheat the oven to 340°F, and line a 12-cup muffin pan with paper muffin cups.

Put the gluten-free flour, potato flour, coconut flour, baking powder, flax meal (if using), and sea salt into a large bowl. Use a wire whisk or sifter to mix them together.

In another bowl, combine the melted coconut oil, agave nectar, vanilla extract, and rice milk. In a small bowl, mix together the baking soda and boiling water and then stir this into the other liquid ingredients.

Pour one-third of the liquid ingredients into the dry and whisk together to make a batter, gradually adding the remaining liquid until all of it is incorporated.

Spoon the batter into the paper cups and bake in the oven for 20–25 minutes, or until a toothpick inserted in the center of a cupcake comes out clean. These cakes are best eaten on the day they are made.

VEGAN VANILLA FROSTING

MAKES: ENOUGH TO FROST 12 CUPCAKES
PREP TIME: 15 MINS + CHILLING
WF · GF · DF · V · Ve

1½ cups **unsweetened soy milk**

scant ½ cup **almond milk powder** (not almond meal)

¼ cup **agave nectar**

2 teaspoons **vanilla extract**

seeds from 1 **vanilla bean**

1½ cups **coconut oil**, melted

2 tablespoons **fresh orange** or **clementine juice**

1 tablespoon **fresh lemon juice**

¼ cup **cashew butter**

We think this frosting might be even better than the traditional butter-and-sugar version. It is the result of weeks spent by Claire testing different dairy- and allergen-free combinations. It is rich, but the coconut oil gives it a sublime melting consistency.

With an immersion blender or in a food processor, combine the soy milk, almond milk powder, agave, and vanilla extract. Blend until smooth. Add the scraped seeds from the vanilla bean.

Combine the melted coconut oil with the orange and lemon juice and add to the mixture gradually, blending until smooth. Add the cashew butter and again blend until smooth.

Chill overnight before using so that the coconut oil solidifies. Remove from the refrigerator 30 minutes–1 hour before using to soften.

═ TIPS ═

For pink frosting, replace ⅔ cup of the soy milk with ⅔ cup pureed and strained raspberries or strawberries. You can play with other natural colors and flavors, such as with Royal Icing (see page 113).

If you can't do soy, substitute rice milk for the soy milk. The texture is not as smooth but the taste is great.

BEN'S VICTORIA SPONGE

SERVES: 8
PREP TIME: 25 MINS + COOLING · COOK TIME: 40 MINS

3 sticks (12 oz) **unsalted butter**, softened, plus extra for greasing

1⅔ cups **superfine sugar**, plus extra for sprinkling

1 teaspoon **vanilla extract**

6 **eggs**

2⅔ cups **all-purpose flour**

2¾ teaspoons **baking powder**

½ cup homemade or good-quality store-bought **raspberry preserves**

2 cups **fresh raspberries** (if in season)

1½ cups **heavy cream**

This is a British traditional layer cake that has stood the test of time. This is the mother of all "teatime" cakes, ideal for an afternoon snack.

Preheat the oven to 325°F. Line two 1-inch round cake pans with parchment paper.

In a large mixing bowl, beat together the soft butter and the sugar until pale and fluffy. Add the vanilla extract and the eggs one at a time, alternating them with 1 tablespoon of flour and beating well after each addition. When all the eggs have been added, add the remaining flour and the baking powder and mix well.

Divide the batter between the 2 pans and bake in the oven for about 40 minutes, or until a toothpick inserted in the center of the cake comes out clean.

Cool the cakes for at least 10 minutes in the pans before turning out onto a wire rack to cool completely.

Just before serving, place one cake on a serving plate and spread the raspberry preserves on top. Whip the cream to soft peaks—just stiff enough to start to hold a shape—and layer that over the preserves, reserving a good dollop for the top of the cake. Sprinkle the raspberries over the cream (saving 2 or 3 for decoration) and finish with the second cake layer. Sprinkle with superfine sugar and put the last dollop of cream on top of the cake. Finish with the raspberries.

═ TIPS ═

This cake is best eaten immediately, but it can be refrigerated in an airtight container for up to 3 days.

You can experiment with all kinds of different fruit fillings.

Try using thick yogurt or sour cream instead of heavy cream.

JOSSY'S LEMON PUDDING DELICIOUS

SERVES: 6
PREP TIME: 20 MINS · COOK TIME: 40 MINS
V

3½ tablespoons **unsalted butter**, at room temperature, plus extra for greasing

generous 1 cup **superfine sugar**

finely grated zest and juice of 2 large **lemons**

4 extra-large **eggs**, separated

generous ⅓ cup **all-purpose flour**

½ teaspoon **baking powder**

scant 1 cup **whole milk**

½ teaspoon **cream of tartar**

confectioners' sugar, for sprinkling (optional)

This dessert was one that Henry's great-grandmother Enid handed down to his mother, Jossy. It was cut out from a newspaper and was called "Lemon Pudding"—next to it Enid had written "delicious!"

Preheat the oven to 350°F and place a roasting pan filled halfway with water on the center shelf. Grease a 1½–2-quart soufflé or other ovenproof dish.

Whisk the butter in a large bowl until soft, then add the sugar and whisk until fluffy. Gradually whisk in the lemon juice, followed by the lemon zest and the egg yolks.

Sift the flour and baking powder onto the mixture and stir it in with a metal spoon, then gradually stir in the milk. Whisk thoroughly until smooth.

In a clean bowl, whisk the egg whites with the cream of tartar using an electric hand-held mixer until they stand in soft peaks. Then, using a metal spoon, fold them gently into the batter, about one-quarter at a time.

Pour the batter into the ovenproof dish and stand it in the roasting pan of water in the oven. Bake for 40 minutes, or slightly less in a convection oven, until risen and golden brown on top.

Serve hot or cold, with confectioners' sugar sifted over the surface, if you want.

BETTER CARROT CAKE

SERVES: 8–10

PREP TIME: 30 MINS + COOLING · COOK TIME: ABOUT 1 HOUR

WF · GF · DF · V · Ve

4 **carrots**, peeled and shredded

⅓ **apple** or **sweet potato**, peeled and shredded

¾ cup **dried, unsweetened shredded coconut**

¼ cup **coconut oil**, melted

¼ cup **sunflower oil**, plus extra for greasing

½ cup **agave nectar**

1½ teaspoons **yacon syrup** (optional)

2 teaspoons **vanilla extract**

¾ cup **chickpea (besan) flour** or ⅔ cup **corn flour**

1 cup **gluten-free all-purpose flour**

1 teaspoon **xanthan gum**

1 teaspoon **baking soda**

½ teaspoon **sea salt**

1½ teaspoons **ground cinnamon**

1 teaspoon **ground ginger**

¾ cup hot **water**

½ teaspoon **mandarin**, **lemon**, or **orange extract**

1 quantity **Vegan Vanilla Frosting** (see page 101)

A beautiful carrot cake made without any dairy, wheat, gluten, or refined sugar. Baking with the ingredients below takes some getting used to—the batter will have a different consistency from a traditional wheat-base cake—but the results are worth the effort. Coconut oil and boiling water make the cake moist. The rice flour gives the cake a fine texture, and the spices and mandarin oil impart a unique flavor.

Preheat the oven to 325°F. Line a 9 x 5 x 3-inch loaf pan with parchment paper.

Combine the carrots, apple or sweet potato, coconut, coconut oil, sunflower oil, agave, yacon syrup, and vanilla in a bowl and set aside.

Combine the dry ingredients in a second bowl and whisk together to evenly distribute them. Whisk in the carrot mixture.

Gradually pour in the hot water and citrus extract and mix to a smooth batter. Pour into the prepared pan.

Bake in the oven for 55–65 minutes, or until a toothpick inserted into the center of the cake comes out clean. Turn out of the loaf pan and let cool completely. Frost with vanilla frosting.

Because there is no gluten in this recipe, the xanthan gum works as a binding agent. If you can't find it, you might find a self-rising gluten-free flour blend that already contains it.

TRIPLE CHOCOLATE FANTASY CAKE

SERVES: 12–15

PREP TIME: 25 MINS + COOLING · COOK TIME: 1 HOUR

V

scant 1 cup **vegetable oil**, plus extra
   for greasing

1¾ cups packed **light brown sugar**

1½ teaspoons **vanilla extract**

3 **eggs**

½ cup **plain yogurt**

1 cup **unsweetened cocoa powder**

scant ½ cup boiling **water**

2¼ cups **all-purpose flour**

1½ teaspoons **baking soda**

½ teaspoon **salt**

FROSTING:

1¾ sticks (7 oz) **unsalted butter**, softened

1⅔ cups **confectioners' sugar**

4–5 tablespoons boiling **water**

1 teaspoon **vanilla extract**

1¼ cups **unsweetened cocoa powder**

TO FINISH:

¼ cup **apricot preserves**

2 **Crunchie chocolate bars**, crumbled

edible glitter (can be found online and in
   speciality cake-decorating stores)

Honeycomb, chocolate, and a hint of apricot make this a dreamy treat. For extra decadence, add crumbled Crunchie chocolate bars between the layers.

Preheat the oven to 325°F. Line two 9-inch cake pans with parchment paper.

Whisk together the oil, sugar, and vanilla. Add the eggs one at a time, mixing well after each addition. Add the yogurt and mix well.

In a small bowl, whisk together the cocoa powder and boiling water until smooth.

Scrape the cocoa paste into the egg mixture and combine into a smooth batter.

Sift together the flour, baking soda, and salt, and beat into the cake batter until just incorporated.

Pour equal amounts into the cake pans and bake in the oven for 55–60 minutes or until a toothpick inserted in the center comes out clean. Let cool in the pans.

Make the frosting. Beat the butter until fluffy. Gradually beat in the confectioners' sugar, then add the boiling water and vanilla extract and beat for 3 minutes.

Add the cocoa powder and beat until fluffy.

To assemble, split each cake into 2 layers. Place the bottom layer on a serving plate and spread it with some of the apricot preserves. Cover with a tablespoon of chocolate frosting and follow with another layer of sponge. Repeat with the remaining layers, then frost the top and sides with the remaining frosting. Decorate with crumbled Crunchie bars and edible glitter.

ZUCCHINI BREAD

1¾ sticks (7 oz) **butter**, plus extra
for greasing

1 cup packed **dark brown sugar**

3 **eggs**

1 **zucchini**, washed and shredded
(skins left on)

1⅔ cups **all-purpose flour**

1 teaspoon **baking powder**

a pinch of **salt**

½ teaspoon **ground cinnamon**

This sweet, dark bread may not be popular outside of the United States, but it is an American staple, perfect for enjoying in the afternoon with a cup of coffee or glass of iced tea. The cinnamon works well with the zucchini, and it's a great alternative to banana bread.

Preheat the oven to 340°F. Line a 9 x 5 x 3-inch loaf pan with parchment paper.

Melt the butter in a small saucepan. Put the brown sugar into a large bowl and whisk in the eggs. Pour the melted butter into the bowl in a steady stream until well mixed in. Stir in the shredded zucchini.

Put the all-purpose flour, baking powder, salt, and cinnamon into another bowl and stir them together.

Add the wet ingredients to the dry ingredients and mix just until incorporated. Pour into the prepared loaf pan and bake for 40–50 minutes, or until springy and a toothpick inserted in the center of the cake comes out clean. Let cool in the pan.

ROYAL ICING

MAKES ENOUGH TO COVER AN 8–10-INCH CAKE

PREP TIME: 10 MINS

WF · GF · DF · V

4 **egg whites**

5¼ cups **confectioners' sugar**

½ cup **water** or **fruit puree**

Spread over a fruitcake or drizzled on cutout cookies, royal icing is an old-fashioned edible decoration that—although incredibly sugary—is as classy as the name suggests. You don't need to reach for artificial colorings (although sometimes we think it's OK and kind of fun). Puree brightly colored fruit to make natural colorings instead (see tip below), or try using turmeric powder for a gorgeous yellow icing with a delicate aniseedy flavor.

Put all the ingredients together in a bowl and use an electric mixer on low speed to mix until combined. Then turn the speed up to medium for about 7 minutes or until thick ribbons form.

You can make the icing softer or looser by adding a little more water.

TIP

Puree fruits that are fresh, ripe, and have a vibrant color by simply blending them to a pulp in a blender. Strain the puree to remove seeds and skin (except in the case of strawberries, which seem to benefit from keeping their little seeds in).

PETRA'S FRUITCAKE

SERVES: 12–15

PREP TIME: 40 MINS + SOAKING AND COOLING · COOK TIME: 3½–4 HOURS

V

1½ cups **golden raisins**

¼ cup **brandy**

generous 1 cup quartered, good-quality **candied cherries**

generous 1 cup good-quality **candied peel**

¾ cup chopped **candied pineapple** or **papaya**

¾ cup chopped **crystallized ginger**

¼ cup chopped **candied angelica**

1 cup chopped **walnuts**

zest and juice of 1 **lemon**

2 sticks (8 oz) **unsalted butter**, softened, plus extra for greasing

generous 1 cup **superfine sugar**

4 **eggs**, at room temperature

1¾ cups **all-purpose flour**

½ teaspoon **salt**

This is another cake from the wonderful Petra (see page 84). This is the cake that she made for her daughters at their christenings, at their weddings, and at the christenings of their own children. Word of its magnificence has spread, and with insane generosity Petra now seems to be in permanent production for friends and family. She varies the recipe a little each year to avoid getting bored. One of the nicest variations was the addition of 3 or 4 sugared apricots from Australia (not the ordinary dried ones). She cut down a little on the sugar and on the other fruit to compensate.

Soak the golden raisins in the brandy for several hours or overnight, then mix in the other fruits and the walnuts.

Prepare a deep 9–10-inch cake pan—one with a loose bottom is best. Line it with 2 layers of parchment paper. To give the cake extra protection, tie a band of paper around the outside of the pan—it should be wide enough to protrude about 1 inch above the rim.

Just before you are ready to start making the cake, add the lemon zest and juice to the fruit.

Preheat the oven to 325°F.

In a large bowl, cream the butter and sugar until pale and fluffy. In a separate bowl, beat the eggs really well with an electric handheld mixer until foamy, thick, and increased in volume—this may take up to 10 minutes, but it is worth it to get the right texture. Add the beaten eggs to the butter mixture a little at a time, beating well after each addition. (If the mixture shows any sign of curdling, beat in a tablespoon of the flour.) Stir in the remaining flour and then the salt.

Now you can stir in the prepared fruit and walnuts, a little at a time.

Turn the batter into the prepared pan and smooth it over with the back of a spoon or a small metal spatula. Put the cake into the oven. After 1½ hours reduce the temperature to 275°F and bake for another 2 hours. After the cake has been in the oven for at least 2 hours, you can look to see if the top is browning too much. If it is, cover it with a double thickness of parchment paper.

The cake is done when it is evenly risen, brown, and has shrunk from the sides of the pan.

Let it cool in the pan, away from drafts, for at least an hour before taking it out. Let it get really cold before storing it in a large pan.

≡ TIPS ≡

The higher the quality of the crystallized or candied fruit the better. Petra buys whole crystallized ones from Harrods in London and chops them up. Golden raisins are essential, because they are so pretty. They can usually be found in Turkish stores.

Petra makes a christening cake by frosting this fruitcake with Royal Icing (see page 113). Instead of aiming for smooth perfection, she frosts this cake coarsely and then covers it with ribbons and little creatures bought from a sewing supply store.

PHOTOGRAPH ON PAGES 116–17 ➡

WARM GOOEY CHOCOLATE CAKES

SERVES: 6–8

PREP TIME: 10 MINS · COOK TIME: 7 MINS

WF · GF · V

6 tablespoons **unsalted butter**, plus extra for greasing

5 oz **semisweet chocolate**

a pinch of **salt**

5 tablespoons **unsweetened cocoa powder**

2 **egg whites**

1 tablespoon **superfine sugar**

Chantilly cream, to serve

One of those chocolate-oozing-out-of-the-middle lava cakes that is not nearly as hard to make as your awestruck guests will assume.

Preheat the oven to 400°F.

Grease 6 or 8 individual ramekins and sprinkle each one with some superfine sugar.

Melt the butter, chocolate, and salt in a large bowl over simmering water. When all is melted, sift in the cocoa powder.

In a separate bowl, whisk together the egg whites and sugar until soft peaks form. Combine with the melted chocolate by folding gently and trying not to knock out too much air.

Spoon the batter into the molds and bake in the oven for just 7 minutes.

TIP

Whatever you do, do not overbake these. They continue to bake slightly as they cool down, so take them out of the oven just before you think they are ready.

You can make the Chantilly cream by adding a small amount of sugar and vanilla extract to whipping cream.

This can also be served with light cream and a splash of Cognac, if you have some around.

A GOOD CHOCOLATE CAKE

SERVES: 8

PREP TIME: 30 MINS + COOLING · COOK TIME: 35 MINS

DF · V · Ve

⅔ cup hot **water**

scant 1 cup **unsweetened cocoa powder**

scant 1 cup **agave syrup**

scant 1 cup **coconut milk**

juice of ½ **lemon**

⅓ cup **sunflower oil**, plus extra
    for greasing

2 teaspoons **vanilla extract**

1⅓ cups **white spelt flour** or
    all-purpose flour

½ teaspoon **baking powder**

1½ teaspoons **baking soda**

a pinch of **salt**

flowers, to decorate (optional),
    insect free and preferably organic

GLAZE:

¼ cup **coconut oil**

7 oz **dairy-free semisweet chocolate**

1 teaspoon **vanilla extract**

¼ cup **agave syrup**

═ TIP ═

Instead of flowers, you could add
some raspberries to the cake and
arrange a few on top for decoration.

A great cake for a children's party if you don't want your house terrorized by children high on sugar and food coloring. It is vegan, but they'll never know it. It also looks ravishing decorated with flowers from the yard.

Preheat the oven to 325°F. Line an 8–9-inch cake pan with parchment paper.

Whisk together the hot water and cocoa powder until smooth. Add the remaining wet ingredients and set aside.

In a large bowl, sift together the flour, baking powder, baking soda, and salt. Pour the wet mixture over the dry and whisk in a circular motion from the center of the bowl, moving outward, to combine. Pour the batter into the cake pan.

Bake in the oven for about 35 minutes, or until a toothpick inserted into the center of the cake comes out clean and the cake is springy to the touch. Let the cake cool for 10 minutes before turning it out onto a wire rack to cool completely.

For the glaze, put all the ingredients into a heatproof bowl, place over a saucepan of barely simmering water to melt, and stir. Move the cake to a serving plate and drizzle the chocolate glaze over it. If you want, decorate with flowers from the yard.

PETRA'S HONEY BREAD

SERVES: 6–8
PREP TIME: 15 MINS + COOLING · COOK TIME: 1¼ HOURS
DF (if oil is used for greasing and butter omitted) · **V**

butter or **oil**, for greasing

1¾ cups **all-purpose flour**

generous ½ cup **superfine sugar**

⅓ cup **honey**, plus extra to glaze

⅔ cup hot **water**

1 tsp **baking soda**

zest of 1 **lemon**

A sweet, soft, wonderfully delicious quick bread. Dangerously addictive with a thick topping of butter.

Preheat the oven to 325°F. Line an 8½ x 4½ x 2½-inch loaf pan with parchment paper.

Mix together the flour and sugar in a large bowl.

In a small saucepan, melt together the honey and the water.

Sprinkle the baking soda over the water mixture and stir. Pour this over the dry ingredients, add the lemon zest, and mix just until incorporated.

Turn the batter into the prepared pan and bake in the oven for 1¼ hours.

Remove from the pan and let cool, then brush with honey and serve thinly sliced.

═ TIP ═
Try replacing the lemon zest with orange or clementine zest.

GUINNESS MALT CAKE

SERVES: 8

PREP TIME: 15 MINS + COOLING · COOK TIME: 1½ HOURS

V (if vegetarian stout is used)

1 cup **Guinness** or other **stout beer**

2¼ sticks (9 oz) **unsalted butter**, plus extra for greasing

1 tablespoon **molasses** or **black treacle**

1 cup packed **dark brown sugar** or **molasses sugar**

generous ¾ cup **unsweeetened cocoa powder**

2 tablespoons **malt powder** (such as Horlicks or Ovaltine)

2 **eggs**

⅔ cup **plain yogurt**

2¼ cups **all-purpose flour**

2 teaspoons **baking soda**

1 cup **superfine sugar**

a pinch of **sea salt**

STOUT AND CREAM CHEESE FROSTING:

scant ⅓ cup **Guinness** or other **stout beer**

4 tablespoons **unsalted butter**, softened

½ cup **cream cheese**, softened

½ teaspoon **vanilla extract**

2⅓ cups **confectioners' sugar**, sifted

A moist and rich cake that marries the flavors of a good stout with malt and dark molasses. The dash of cocoa powder adds to the beautiful color. This cake will keep well for up to a week.

Preheat the oven to 325°F. Line a 9 x 5 x 3-inch loaf pan with parchment paper.

Put the Guinness, butter, molasses, and brown sugar into a small saucepan and melt over medium heat. Whisk in the cocoa and malt, then remove from the heat and let cool a little.

In a large bowl, whisk together the eggs and yogurt, then add the stout mixture.

Sift together the remaining dry ingredients into the bowl and whisk together to combine. Pour into the prepared pan and bake in the oven for about 1¼ hours, or until a toothpick inserted into the center of the cake comes out clean. Cool the cake completely in the pan.

While the cake is cooling, make the frosting: put the Guinness in a small saucepan and bring to a boil. Boil for 10–15 minutes or until the beer has reduced by half its volume. Pour into a container and put it into the refrigerator to cool down.

In a mixing bowl, beat the soft butter until creamy and light. Add the cream cheese and beat until smooth. Add the vanilla and the sifted confectioners' sugar and beat well. Now add the cooled, reduced Guinness and beat until creamy and light. Turn out the cake from of its pan and spread the frosting on top.

LEON'S BIRTHDAY CAKE

SERVES: 12–15

PREP TIME: 40 MINS + COOLING AND CHILLING · COOK TIME: 50 MINS

V

1 stick (4 oz) **unsalted butter**, softened,
   plus extra for greasing

1 cup **superfine sugar**

3 **eggs**

½ teaspoon **salt**

2⅓ cups **all-purpose flour**

2½ teaspoons **baking powder**

¾ cup **coconut milk**

SYRUP:

⅔ cup **coconut milk**

½ cup **sugar**

½ teaspoon **vanilla extract**

a pinch of **salt**

FILLING:

scant 1 cup **coconut milk**

½ cup **superfine sugar**

⅓ cup **water**

2 tablespoons **cornstarch**, mixed
   with ¼ cup **water**

a pinch of **salt**

TO DECORATE:

1¼ cups **whipped cream**

1¼ cups **coconut shavings**

This cake looks crazy—like a gigantic, delicious powder puff, or a Bounty bar turned inside out. It tastes amazing, too. The coconut filling has the texture and flavor of fresh coconut flesh.

Preheat the oven to 350°F. Line a 9-inch cake pan with parchment paper.

Cream the butter and sugar until almost white and fluffy. Add the eggs and salt and mix until completely incorporated. Add half the flour and the baking powder until just combined. Add the coconut milk and mix until combined. Then add the remaining flour and mix well.

Pour the batter into the cake pan and smooth the top. Bake for 40–50 minutes, until a toothpick inserted into the center of the cake comes out clean and the cake springs back to the touch. Let the cake cool completely in the pan.

To make the filling, put the coconut milk, sugar, and water into a heavy saucepan and put over medium heat. Stir to dissolve the sugar, then increase the heat to high. Add the cornstarch mixture to the pan with the salt and whisk until thick. Pour the mixture into a bowl and press plastic wrap over the surface. Let it cool, then chill in the refrigerator for at least 2 hours.

To make the syrup, heat all the syrup ingredients together in a small saucepan and cook over medium heat for 5 minutes.

Slice the cooled cake into 3 layers. Drizzle with the syrup, and sandwich with the coconut filling. Cover the top and sides of the cake with whipped cream and sprinkle with generous amounts of coconut shavings.

RUBY'S PEPPERMINT CREAM CUPCAKES

MAKES: 12 CUPCAKES
PREP TIME: 30 MINS + COOLING · COOK TIME: 23 MINS
WF · GF · DF · V · Ve

scant 1½ cups **gluten-free flour**

¾ cup **unsweetened cocoa powder**

1 tablespoon **baking powder**

1 teaspoon **fine sea salt**

½ cup **sunflower oil**

1 cup **superfine sugar**

1 teaspoon **vanilla extract**

2 teaspoons **peppermint oil**

½ cup **applesauce**

scant 1 cup hot **water**

FROSTING:

¼ cup **vegan dairy-free spread**

2⅔ cups **confectioners' sugar**, sifted

½ teaspoon **vanilla extract**

1 teaspoon **peppermint oil**

a splash of **nondairy milk** of choice
(such as soy, oat, coconut, or almond)

TO DECORATE:

vegan chocolate, melted, for drizzling

12 **fresh mint sprigs** (optional)

Ruby started her vegan bakery with a stall in Greenwich Market, and now her cakes are a cult favorite across London. This particular one is John, our CEO's, favorite cake in the world. And he isn't even vegan.

Preheat the oven to 340°F and line a 12-cup muffin pan with cupcake liners.

In a large bowl, sift together the flour, cocoa, baking powder, and salt.

In a separate bowl, mix together the oil, sugar, vanilla, peppermint oil, and applesauce, until well combined. Add the hot water, then gradually add the dry ingredients to the wet, mixing between each addition until well combined.

Divide the batter evenly among the 12 cupcake liners and bake in the oven for 23 minutes, until they have a shiny crust and a toothpick inserted comes out clean. Let cool in the pan before decorating.

To make the frosting, beat the vegan spread in a freestanding mixer or with an electric handheld mixer until smooth. Gradually add the confectioners' sugar in small increments, beating as you work. Add the vanilla extract and peppermint oil, then gradually add small drops of milk, beating between each addition, until the frosting is soft and smooth. Chill until the frosting has firmed up a little.

Decorate the cupcakes with the frosting, as desired. Top with a drizzle of melted chocolate and a fresh mint sprig if eating on the same day.

TECHNICOLOR DREAM CAKE

SERVES: 10–12

PREP TIME: 25 MINS + COOLING · COOK TIME: 50 MINS

V

2½ cups **all-purpose flour**

½ teaspoon **salt**

4 teaspoons **baking powder**

1¾ sticks (7 oz) **unsalted butter**, softened, plus extra for greasing

2 cups **sugar**

1 teaspoon **vanilla extract**

4 **eggs**, separated

scant 1 cup **milk**

fresh fruit, to decorate

FOR EACH OF THE 4 LAYERS OF FROSTING:

3 tablespoons **fresh fruit puree**, strained (we used raspberry, quince, and strawberry), or a pinch of **turmeric**

2 tablespoons **unsalted butter**, softened

1¼ cups **confectioners' sugar**

lemon juice or **vanilla extract**

TIP

To make the frosting, strain the fruit puree and set aside. In a medium bowl, beat the butter and sugar until light and fluffy. Add the fruit puree or turmeric, then taste. A little lemon juice or vanilla can balance the flavors of your frosting.

A really fun cake to make, and lurid enough—despite the natural colors—to satisfy any child. The idea came from an old cake book Claire picked up at a thrift shop.

Preheat the oven to 325°F. Line two 9-inch cake pans with parchment paper.

In a large bowl, sift together the flour, salt, and baking powder and set aside.

Cream the butter and sugar until fluffy. Add the vanilla, then the egg yolks one at a time, mixing well after each addition. Add half the milk and mix well. Add half the flour mixture and combine. Repeat with the remaining milk and flour.

Whisk the egg whites in a clean bowl until soft peaks form. Stir one-third of the egg whites into the cake mixture to lighten the batter and then fold in the remainder, being careful not to knock out too much air in the process.

Divide the batter between the pans and bake in the oven for 45–50 minutes or until a toothpick inserted into the center of the cake comes out clean. Let the cakes cool for 10 minutes before taking them out of the pans and letting them cool completely on a wire rack.

Slice each layer in two and place the bottom of one on a cake stand. Spread with the first frosting flavor, then continue to stack up the layers. Top with fresh fruit.

BARS, COOKIES & BUNS

CUTOUT COOKIES

MAKES: 24 COOKIES, DEPENDING ON SIZE
PREP TIME: 15 MINS + CHILLING AND COOLING · COOK TIME: 10–12 MINS
V

2 sticks (8 oz) **unsalted butter**, softened

2 cups **superfine sugar**

2 **eggs**

1 teaspoon **vanilla extract**

4½ cups **all-purpose flour**, plus extra for dusting

1 teaspoon **baking powder**

a pinch of **salt**

Royal Icing (see page 113)

You need the right kind of dough to make cutout cookies—one that holds its shape during cooking. These cookies should be a cornerstone of your baking repertoire, especially if you have young children—they're both tasty and a great way to keep the kids entertained.

With an electric handheld mixer, beat the softened butter with the superfine sugar until light, pale, and fluffy.

Add the eggs, one by one, then the vanilla extract.

Put the flour into a separate bowl and whisk in the baking powder and salt. Add half of this to the creamed mixture and beat on low speed until just combined.

Add the remaining flour mixture and beat again to combine well.

Divide the dough in half and wrap each ball in plastic wrap. You could freeze one ball for another time, if you want. Chill for about 2 hours or overnight before using.

When ready to make the cookies, preheat the oven to 350°F. Line a couple of baking sheets with parchment paper.

Lightly dust a work surface with flour, then roll out the dough to about ¼ inch thick. Cut out shapes with your cookie cutters and transfer the cookies to your prepared baking sheets. Chill for 15–20 minutes, then bake for 10–12 minutes or until just starting to turn golden. Transfer to a wire rack and let cool completely.

Decorate the cookies with Royal Icing and let stand overnight to dry.

Store in an airtight container for up to a week.

TIP

Try adding flavors to the cookies for variation. You can try the variations suggested on page 168, or add lemon zest, cinnamon, or other spices you like. Henry is fond of ground cardamom seeds for a scented flavor.

VIOLET COCONUT MACAROONS

MAKES: 12 MACAROONS
PREP TIME: 15 MINS + COOLING · COOK TIME: 20 MINS
WF · GF · DF

3 **egg whites**

¾ cup **superfine sugar**

a pinch of **salt**

2 teaspoons **honey**

2 cups **unsweetened, dried shredded coconut**

½ teaspoon **vanilla extract** (optional)

There is a sublime crispy gooiness to these cookies that makes them like nothing else on earth. Warning: They are addictive. Violet is the name of Claire's bakery and shop on Wilton Way and her stall at Broadway Market, both in Hackney, London.

Preheat the oven to 300°F. Line a baking sheet with parchment paper.

Combine the egg whites, superfine sugar, salt, honey, and dried coconut in a large saucepan over medium heat.

Stir the mixture constantly until everything is dissolved and it just begins to scorch on the bottom. Remove the pan from the heat and stir in the vanilla.

Let the mixture cool completely, then use an ice cream scoop (about ¼ cup) to scoop out 12 even macaroons and place them on the baking sheet.

Bake in the oven for 10–15 minutes or until golden and set. Let the macaroons cool completely before peeling off the paper.

= TIP =

The key to getting these macaroons just right is to stir the ingredients in the pan until they begin to dry out.

NANA GOY'S CRANBERRY OAT BARS

MAKES: 16 OAT BARS

PREP TIME: 10 MINS + COOLING · COOK TIME: 30–35 MINS

WF · GF · V

⅓ cup **dried cranberries**

¼ cup **golden syrup** or **dark corn syrup**

1½ sticks (6 oz) **butter**, plus extra for greasing

½ cup **superfine sugar**

2¾ cups **gluten-free rolled oats**

These are moist and deliciously oaty like a good oat bar should be. We love them with dried cranberries, but you could use any dried fruits you want (see tip below).

Preheat the oven to 350°F and grease an 8-inch square baking pan.

Put the cranberries into a bowl and cover with boiling water. Let them soak for a few minutes until they are plump and rehydrated. Drain away the water and coarsely chop any that are particularly large.

Melt the syrup, butter, and sugar together in a large saucepan over low heat until the sugar has dissolved, then stir in the oats. Add all but a small handful of the cranberries and stir thoroughly.

Transfer the oat bar mixture into the pan and smooth it down with a spatula. Sprinkle the remaining cranberries on top. Bake in the oven for 30–35 minutes, until golden. Mark into squares while still warm, and remove from the pan when cool.

= TIP =

For a fruity hit, try making these with chopped dates instead of the cranberries. Add a handful of nuts and seeds to the mixture to add another dimension to your oat bars.

ELISABETH'S LEMON BARS

MAKES: 8–10 BARS

PREP TIME: 30 MINS · COOK TIME: 45 MINS–1 HOUR

V

4 **eggs**, beaten

1¾ cups **sugar**

½ cup **fresh lemon juice** (Meyer or
Amalfi, if possible)

½ teaspoon grated **lemon zest** (Meyer
or Amalfi, if possible)

¼ cup **all-purpose flour**

1 teaspoon **baking powder**

confectioners' sugar, to finish

SHORTBREAD LAYER:

2¼ cups **all-purpose flour**

⅔ cup **confectioners' sugar**

1 teaspoon **salt**

2 sticks (8 oz) **unsalted butter**, cold

Sweet and gooey, with a sharp finish. An indulgent treat.

Preheat the oven to 340°F.

First make the shortbread layer. Combine the flour, confectioners' sugar, salt, and cold butter in a food processor and mix until crumbly. If you don't have a food processor, cut the butter up with two knives, the back of a fork, or an old-fashioned pastry cutter.

Be careful not to let the butter get too warm either in the appliance or in your hands, because it changes the texture. Mix just until the dough forms a ball.

Press the dough into a 12 x 8-inch baking pan.

Bake in the oven for 20–25 minutes or until golden and set, then let cool slightly while you get on with the topping.

Put the eggs into a bowl with the sugar, lemon juice, and lemon zest. In a separate bowl, sift together the flour and baking powder. Add to the egg mixture and stir to combine. Spread onto the cooled shortbread crust and return to the oven for 25–30 minutes or until just set.

Cool completely in the pan. Sprinkle with confectioners' sugar and cut into bars. These will keep well in an airtight container for up to 3 days.

═ TIP ═

Sprinkle with lavender flowers if you have them growing in your yard.

CHERRY & ALMOND SLICE

. . . .

MAKES: 14 SLICES
PREP TIME: 20 MINS + COOLING · COOK TIME: 25–30 MINS
WF · GF · V

. . . .

1¾ sticks (6 oz) **salted butter**, at
room temperature

1 cup **superfine sugar**

2 extra-large **eggs**

¼ teaspoon **almond extract**

1½ cups **cornmeal**

1 cup **almond meal**

¼ teaspoon **gluten-free baking powder**

1¼ cups pitted fresh **sour cherries**
(frozen will also work)

¼ cup **pistachios**, coarsely chopped

4 teaspoons **milk**

4 teaspoons **lemon juice**

½ cup **confectioners' sugar**

This cake takes the title of "most samples ever ordered to our office before launch." Which is to say, we may have ordered a few more samples than necessary, because we couldn't stop snacking on it. This cake is made with whole sour cherries baked into a sponge with lemon juice and almond flour, making it taste like the lovechild of a lemon drizzle and a cherry-almond cake. Perfect for the indecisive among us.

. . . .

Preheat the oven to 350°F. Grease a deep, 10-inch square baking pan and line with parchment paper.

In a large bowl, beat together the butter and sugar until fluffy and smooth. Beat in the eggs one at a time, then beat in the almond extract until well combined. Add the cornmeal, almond meal, and baking powder and fold in until well combined.

Scrape out the batter into the lined pan and evenly sprinkle the sour cherries and pistachios over the surface of the batter, reserving about one-third of the pistachios for decorating.

Bake for 25–30 minutes, until just beginning to turn pale golden. Remove from the oven and let cool in the pan.

Meanwhile, combine the milk, lemon juice, and confectioners' sugar in a small saucepan and heat, whisking all the time, until the syrup is warm and no lumps of sugar remain.

Brush the hot syrup over the still-warm cake and sprinkle the reserved pistachios over the surface. Let the cake completely cool and set, then turn out of the pan and cut into slices or squares.

SPELT HOT CROSS BUNS

MAKES: 12 ROLLS

PREP TIME: 50 MINS + RISING · COOK TIME: 15 MINS

DF · V · Ve (if made with egg substitute)

4½ teaspoons **instant yeast**

scant 1 cup **rice milk**, warmed slightly, plus extra for brushing

scant 1 cup **agave nectar**

2¼ cups **whole-grain spelt flour**

2¼ cups **while spelt flour**

1 teaspoon **salt**

½ teaspoon **ground allspice**

½ teaspoon freshly grated **nutmeg**

1 teaspoon **ground cinnamon**

½ cup **dried currants**

½ cup **golden raisins**

zest of 1 **orange**

1 **egg** or **egg substitute**

¼ cup **coconut oil**, melted

CROSSES:

⅔ cup **spelt flour**

1 tablespoon **water**

WASH:

⅓ cup **water**

scant ½ cup **agave nectar**

Wholesome and delicious. These buns are less sweet than most hot cross buns but just as festive. Toast them and spread with butter or coconut oil.

Preheat the oven to 425°F. Line 2 baking sheets with parchment paper.

Dissolve the yeast in the warm rice milk with the agave nectar and set aside.

In a separate bowl, combine the flours, salt, spices, currants, golden raisins, and zest.

Add the egg or egg substitute and the coconut oil to the milk mixture, then pour all of this over the dry ingredients. Stir the dough to combine and then cover and let rest for about 20 minutes.

Turn out the dough onto a floured surface and knead for 10–12 minutes, until silky. Put it back into the bowl and cover with a clean cloth. Let rise in a warm place until the dough has nearly doubled in bulk. This should take about 3 hours.

Divide the dough into 12 pieces. Form each piece into a ball and place on the prepared baking sheets about ¾ inch apart. Let the buns rise on the baking sheets for 30–45 minutes while you prepare the crosses.

Put the flour for the crosses into a small bowl and add water to make a paste. Brush the risen buns with a little rice milk. Use a pastry bag with a small round nozzle (or make one out of paper) to pipe the paste in a cross over each bun. Bake in the oven for about 15 minutes or until golden brown.

While the rolls are baking, make the wash by heating the water and agave nectar in a small saucepan. As soon as the buns come out of the oven, brush them with the wash. Serve warm or toasted.

GOOD SCONES

MAKES: 12 SCONES

PREP TIME: 20 MINS + RESTING AND COOLING · COOK TIME: 25 MINS

DF · V · Ve (if cream substitute is used)

⅔ cup **gluten-free all-purpose flour**

scant 1 cup **white spelt flour**

2¾ teaspoons **gluten-free baking powder**

a large pinch of **salt**

¼ cup **coconut oil**, melted, or **sunflower oil**

2 tablespoons **maple syrup**

1 tablespoon **vanilla extract**

⅓ cup hot **water**

¼ cup **rice milk**

clotted cream or **clotted cream substitute** (see tip) and **strawberry jam**, to serve

These scones are made with of lot of alternative ingredients that make them healthier. But we like the idea of eating them the traditional British way with clotted cream and strawberry jam anyway.

Measure all the dry ingredients into a large bowl. In a small saucepan, melt the coconut oil and let it cool slightly. Pour the oil over the dry ingredients and toss together with a fork.

Mix the remaining ingredients, except the cream and jam, into the dry ingredients just until combined. Don't overwork it.

Let the dough rest for 10 minutes. Meanwhile, line a baking sheet with parchment paper and preheat the oven to 350°F.

Roll out the dough to about ¾ inch thick. Use a cookie cutter or the rim of a glass to cut out about 12 round disks.

Place the scones on the baking sheet and bake in the oven for 20–25 minutes.

When they are ready and firm to the touch, remove them from the oven and place on a cooling rack. Cool completely before splitting open and filling with the cream and jam.

═ TIPS ═

For wheat- and gluten- free scones, swap the spelt flour for chickpea (gram) flour or use more gluten-free all-purpose flour.

To make a clotted cream substitute, try mixing 1 cup marscarpone cheese with ⅓ cup heavy cream until thick and stiff, then chill before using.

ECCLES CAKES

1 stick (4 oz) **unsalted butter**

1½ cups packed **dark brown sugar**

3 cups **dried currants**

2 teaspoons **ground cinnamon**

½ teaspoon **nutmeg**, freshly grated

zest of 1 **orange**

1 (12-oz) package **puff dough**

all-purpose flour, for dusting

1 **egg** or **egg yolk**, for glazing

1 tablespoon **light cream**

These Lancashire dried currant cakes are a quintessentially English treat, and they are amazing served with a crumbly, mild Lancashire cheese. But only eat one: They are so rich that they were banned by the Puritans lest they agitate ungodly humors.

Melt the butter with the sugar, currants, cinnamon, nutmeg, and orange zest.

Chill for at least 1 hour, then divide the mixture into 12 balls. Preheat the oven to 350°F and line a baking sheet with parchment paper.

Roll out the puff dough on a floured surface and cut into 12 squares, 4 inches across. Place a ball of filling on each one, then bring the edges together around the ball of filling and pinch to seal so the filling does not escape when cooking.

Place, seam side down, on the baking sheet and chill for 10 minutes.

In a small bowl, mix the egg or egg yolk and cream together with a fork to make an egg wash. Brush the cakes with the egg wash, then use scissors to snip 3 small holes in the top of each cake. Bake in the oven for 20–25 minutes, until golden and risen. Transfer to a wire rack to cool.

= TIP =

Try adding a drop of rum to the currant mixture—a trick apparently used to help preserve them when the Lancastrians exported them in the early nineteenth century.

MAGGIE'S BEST CHOCOLATE CHIP COOKIES

MAKES: 24 COOKIES

PREP TIME: 15 MINS · COOK TIME: 11 MINS

WF · GF · V

1¾ cups **gluten-free all-purpose flour**

2 teaspoons **gluten-free baking powder**

½ teaspoon **sea salt**

1 cup **semisweet chocolate chips**
   or **chunks**

¼ cup **agave nectar**

scant 1 cup **maple syrup**

1 stick (4 oz) **unsalted butter**, melted

1 tablespoon **vanilla extract**

sea salt, for sprinkling (optional)

Gooey, chocolaty, but without the wheat flour or refined sugar.

Preheat the oven to 350°F. Line a baking sheet with parchment paper.

Mix together all the dry ingredients in a medium bowl (including the chocolate chips or chunks).

Mix together all the wet ingredients in a small bowl.

Add the wet ingredients to the dry ingredients and stir until they are well combined, but do not overmix.

Drop spoonfuls of the cookie dough onto the prepared baking sheet. Lightly sprinkle with sea salt, if you want.

Bake in the oven for only 11 minutes, and let the cookies cool on the baking sheet for 1 minute before transferring to a cooling rack.

═ TIPS ═

Following the baking time directions exactly will give you the perfect gooey texture.

If you can't get hold of gluten-free flour and you don't mind the gluten, 2 cups of normal flour can be substituted.

BAR OF GOOD THINGS

MAKES: 8 BARS

PREP TIME: 20 MINS + SOAKING · COOK TIME: 2 HOURS

WF · GF · DF · V · Ve

generous 1 cup **sesame seeds**,
   preferably soaked and dried

generous ¾ cup **cashew nuts**,
   finely chopped

a pinch of **sea salt**

2 tablespoons **brown rice syrup**

2 tablespoons **tahini**

2 tablespoons **yacon syrup**

2 teaspoons **lemon zest**

½ cup shelled **roasted, salted pistachios**,
   coarsely chopped

½ cup chopped **dried apricots**

FIG PASTE:

¼ cup **water**

1 teaspoon **vanilla extract**

⅓ cup **dried figs**

1¼ teaspoons **ground ginger**

¼ teaspoon **ground cumin**

COATING:

⅔ cup **sesame seeds**, lightly toasted

═ TIP ═

The yacon syrup can be replaced with
more brown rice syrup or agave nectar.

Well, you are what you eat.

Preheat the oven to 225°F. Line a 12 x 8-inch baking pan with parchment paper.

For the fig paste, heat the water with the vanilla in a small saucepan and pour over the dried figs. Let soak for 15 minutes, then blend with the ginger and cumin to form a paste.

Meanwhile, mix the sesame seeds, cashews, and salt in a medium bowl.

Mix the brown rice syrup, tahini, yacon, and lemon zest in a small bowl and stir in the fig paste.

Add the wet ingredients to the dry ingredients and mix well (this is easiest done with your hands, because the mixture should be stiff). Then fold in the pistachios and apricots.

Sprinkle half the sesame seeds for coating into the prepared baking pan, then press the mixture evenly on top to about ½ inch thick. Sprinkle with the remaining seeds.

Bake in the oven for 1 hour, then flip it over, put it back in the pan, and bake for another 1 hour. Let cool in the pan. Cut into bars and keep in an airtight container.

BETTER BROWNIE

MAKES: 12 LARGE BROWNIES
PREP TIME: 25 MINS · COOK TIME: 35 MINS
WF · GF · V

1½ sticks (6 oz) **unsalted butter**,
    plus extra for greasing

7 oz **semisweet chocolate**

1 **orange**

2 teaspoons **espresso** or **strong coffee**

½ cup **whole almonds** (skins on)

4 **eggs**

1 cup **almond meal**

1 cup **semisweet chocolate chunks**

1 cup **bittersweet chocolate chunks**

⅔ cup packed **brown sugar**

a pinch of **sea salt**

3–4 drops of **vanilla extract**

We have been selling these brownies at LEON since we opened our first restaurant in London's Carnaby Street in 2004. They were developed by Emma Goss-Custard, one of our favorite bakers. Her stroke of genius was to add some strong espresso and orange zest, with their bitter and citrus notes contrasting perfectly against the sweet chocolate chunks.

Preheat the oven to 350°F. Generously grease a 12 x 8 x 5-inch baking pan or one of similar dimensions.

Melt the butter in a small saucepan and let it cool slightly.

In a separate bowl, melt the semisweet chocolate in a heatproof bowl set over a saucepan of hot water, stirring well to make sure that it is properly melted, and being careful not to burn it. Finely grate the orange zest directly into the melted chocolate to catch the oils that are released during the zesting process.

Add the coffee to the melted butter.

On another baking pan, spread out the whole almonds and toast in the oven for 10 minutes, then coarsely chop.

Crack the eggs into a large mixing bowl. Add the almond meal, chopped almonds, all the chocolate chunks, and the sugar. Stir in the salt and vanilla, followed by the melted chocolate-and-butter mixture.

Mix well until creamy and thickened, but do not overmix, because too much air will cause the brownie to crumble when baked.

Spoon the batter into the prepared baking pan and place in the oven for about 20–25 minutes. Be careful to avoid overbaking the brownies. They are ready when the edges are slightly crusty but the middle is still soft.

Remove from the oven and let cool in the pan.

TIP

You can replace the brown sugar with 150g of fructose. Fructose turns a much darker colour when baked than sugar. The brownie develops a glossy sheen and will not look cooked, when in fact it is. Resist the temptation to cook it for too long.

PHOTOGRAPH ON PAGES 156–57 ➞

LISE'S CHERRY ALMOND COOKIES

1¾ sticks (7 oz) **salted butter**, softened, plus extra for greasing

1 cup packed **brown sugar**

2 medium **eggs**

1 cup **all-purpose flour**

½ teaspoon **baking soda**

2 cups **rolled oats**

1 cup **dried sour cherries**

½ cup **slivered almonds**

½ cup **chocolate chips**

The recipe below is based on Lise's oat and raisin cookies, but with a sweet summer twist to it. If you want to make the original version, just replace the chocolate chips, cherries, and almonds with raisins.

Preheat the oven to 350°F. Grease several large baking sheets or line them with parchment paper.

Cream together the butter and sugar, then add the eggs one at a time, and beat until light and fluffy.

In another bowl, combine the flour, baking soda, oats, cherries, slivered almonds, and chocolate chips. Add to the butter mixture, being careful to avoid overmixing the dough.

Use an ice cream scoop or 2 tablespoons to scoop 2-inch balls of dough onto the baking sheets. Space the balls about 5 inches apart. Each cookie will spread to about 4 inches. If your dough is cold, the cookies will not spread as well, in which case you will need to flatten them a little with the palm of your hand before baking.

Bake in the oven for 10–12 minutes, or until golden (you may need to bake them in batches). The cookies will be soft when you take them out, but they will become firm as they cool down. Let them rest on the baking sheets for a few minutes before transferring them to a wire rack to cool completely. Store in an airtight container.

LEMON, ZUCCHINI & CORNMEAL SHEET CAKE

MAKES: 16 SLICES
PREP TIME: 20 MINS · COOK TIME: 25–30 MINS
WF · GF · DF · V

1 cup **superfine sugar**

zest of 2 **lemons**

2 extra-large **eggs**

scant 1 cup **canola oil**

scant 1 cup **cornmeal**

1 cup **almond meal**

1 teaspoon **gluten-free baking powder**

¼ teaspoon **salt**

1⅓ cups shredded **zucchini**

3 tablespoons finely chopped
   shelled **pistachios**

dried rose petals, for sprinkling

LEMON SYRUP:

¼ cup **lemon juice**

¼ cup **superfine sugar**

The first disclaimer we need to make about this cake is: No, you can't taste the zucchini. The second is: It's really, really good. The cornmeal layer soaks up all of the lemon syrup, making it extra (sorry) moist, and the rose petals and pistachios sprinkled on top give it a fragrant, nutty finish. A recipe from our friend, Mike Smart.

Preheat the oven to 350°F. Grease a deep, 10-inch square baking pan and line with parchment paper.

In a large bowl, beat together the sugar and lemon zest, until the sugar is the consistency of damp sand. Add the eggs and oil to the mixture and beat until smooth and well combined. Add the cornmeal, almond meal, baking powder, and salt and fold in until well combined, then fold in the zucchini.

Scrape the batter into the lined pan and bake for 25–30 minutes, until just beginning to turn pale golden.

Meanwhile, make the syrup. In a small saucepan, heat the lemon juice and superfine sugar, stirring until the sugar has completely dissolved and a warm syrup has formed.

Evenly sprinkle the chopped pistachios and dried rose petals over the surface of the still-warm cake, then use a spoon to drizzle over the warm lemon syrup.

Let the cake cool completely, then turn out of the pan and cut into 16 squares.

TIP

You could experiment with the flavors in this recipe by substituting the lemon zest and juice with equal quantities of another citrus fruit, such as orange or grapefruit.

PHOTOGRAPH ON PAGES 162–63 ➜

OAT & CRANBERRY COOKIES

MAKES: 24 COOKIES
PREP TIME: 20 MINS, PLUS RESTING (OPTIONAL) · COOK TIME: 20–23 MINS
V

⅔ cup packed **light brown sugar**

⅓ cup **superfine sugar**

2 sticks (8 oz) **unsalted butter**

scant 1⅔ cups **all-purpose flour**

½ teaspoon **ground cinnamon**

1 teaspoon **baking powder**

1 teaspoon **fine sea salt**

2 **eggs**

1⅓ cups **rolled oats**

⅓ cup **golden raisins**

⅓ cup **dried cranberries**

⅓ cup **hazelnuts**

½ cup shelled **pistachios**

The perfect ratio of crispy edges to gooey center.

Preheat the oven to 325°F and line 2 baking sheets with parchment paper.

In a large bowl, combine the sugars and butter and beat until fluffy.

In a separate bowl, sift together the flour, cinnamon, baking powder, and ½ teaspoon of the salt, then add into the butter mixture and mix to combine. Add the eggs one at a time, mixing thoroughly after each addition, until you have a dough that is sticky and soft.

In the same bowl that held the flour, combine the oats, dried fruits, and nuts with the remaining ½ teaspoon of salt, then add to the dough mixture and give it one final mix to combine. If you have time, transfer the dough to the refrigerator to rest for 1 hour (this will help prevent the cookies from spreading too much in the oven).

Scoop heaping tablespoons of the dough onto the prepared baking sheets, making sure they are well spaced to allow for spreading. Bake for 20–23 minutes, until golden. Let the cookies cool on the sheets for 2–3 minutes, before transferring to a wire rack to cool completely.

ALMOND, DATE & OAT MUFFINS

MAKES: 12 MUFFINS
PREP TIME: 20 MINS · COOK TIME: 25 MINS
V

⅔ cup **whole almonds** (skins on)

1¾ sticks (7 oz) **unsalted butter**, melted

⅓ cup packed **light brown sugar**

2 cups **oat bran**

1 cup **rolled oats**, plus extra for sprinkling

2 cups **fine spelt flour**

½ teaspoon **salt**

1½ teaspoons **baking soda**

2 **eggs**

1½ cups **plain yogurt**

1¾ cups pitted chopped **dates**

zest of 1 **orange**

A nutty, semisweet breakfast muffin made with spelt flour, which is better for you than other varieties of wheat, and also gives it its distinctive texture and flavor.

Preheat the oven to 340°F. Grease a 12-cup muffin pan or line it with paper liners.

Spread the almonds out on a baking sheet and toast in the oven for 5–7 minutes or until golden.

Melt the butter and sugar in a small saucepan and set aside to cool slightly.

In a large bowl, mix together the oat bran, rolled oats, spelt flour, salt, and baking soda. Coarsely chop the toasted almonds and stir them into the dry ingredients.

In a separate bowl, whisk together the eggs and yogurt and stir in the dates and orange zest. Whisk in the melted butter and sugar and pour all of the wet mixture over the dry ingredients. Mix just until combined.

Spoon the batter into the muffin pan and bake in the oven for 20–25 minutes, until the muffins are golden.

= TIP =

You could also make these muffins with dates that have been soaked in juice or alcohol.

HALLOWEEN COOKIES

1 quantity **Cutout Cookies** (see page 135)
writing icing tubes, for drawing
sprinkles, to decorate

FOR EACH COLOR ICING:
1 tablespoon **water**
a few drops of **food coloring**
confectioners' sugar

Make the Cutout Cookies on page 135, adding ½ teaspoon of pumpkin pie spice to make some autumnal lightly spiced cookies, or to make them chocolaty, substitute ¾ cup unsweetened cocoa powder for ½ cup flour.

Make a few colored icings in different bowls by mixing the water and food coloring, then adding confectioners' sugar until the icing is thick and smooth (not too runny).

Using the icings as backgrounds and the writing icing tubes for the detail, unleash the creative beast in you. If you're making these with children, you really should let them do the decorating. Lay out plenty of little bowls filled with sugary things to stick onto the icing—sprinkles, silver sugar balls, sugar-coated chocolate candies, whatever—and let them go mental.

DESSERTS

PAVLOVA

SERVES: 6

PREP TIME: 20 MINS + COOLING · COOK TIME: 2 HOURS

WF · GF · V

3 **egg whites**

¼ teaspoon **salt**

½ teaspoon **white wine vinegar**

½ teaspoon **vanilla extract**

1½ cups **superfine sugar**

1½ teaspoons **cornstarch**

TO SERVE:

3 tablespoons **raspberry preserves**

1 cup **heavy cream**, lightly whipped

4 cups hulled **strawberries**

2 tablespoons **superfine sugar**

3 **passion fruit**

There are hundreds of ways to dress a pavlova—a meringue shell topped with whipped cream and fruit—but this is our favorite: simple, clean, and drizzled with the sharp, juicy pulp of passion fruit. We like to use individual meringues to make the recipients feel extra special.

Preheat the oven to 250°F. Line a baking sheet with parchment paper.

Using an electric handheld mixer, beat the egg whites, salt, vinegar, and vanilla on high speed until soft peaks form.

Whisk 1 cup of the sugar and the cornstarch together by hand and add half to the frothy egg whites. Use the electric handheld mixer to whip until stiff, then add the remaining half. Whisk until stiff again, then add the remaining ½ cup of sugar. Whisk until smooth and glossy.

Spoon 6 large swoops of the meringue onto the baking sheet 1½ inches apart.

Bake in the oven for about 2 hours, then check the meringues. Remove from the oven when dry and firm. It should be possible to gently peel them off the paper. If they stick to the paper, they're not ready. Cool completely when cooked.

To assemble, place the meringues on a large serving plate or individual plates. Put a spoonful of raspberry preserves on each and then a generous dollop of cream.

Quarter the strawberries and toss with the sugar. Let macerate for a few minutes while you halve the passion fruits. To save time, you can prepare the strawberries up to 2 hours in advance and keep them in the refrigerator.

Stir the strawberries and divide among the pavlovas. Scoop out half a passion fruit onto each and serve.

≡ TIPS ≡

Making meringue can be intimidating, but it doesn't need to be when you know a few tricks and you have the right tools. An electric handheld or free-standing mixer will always make it easier to make meringues. Meringue can take an incredible amount of beating (unlike cream) so it is hard to overdo it. The salt and cornstarch help to stabilize the whites and keep them from "breaking."

Meringues can be made up to 5 days in advance and kept in an airtight container.

The trick to making successful meringues is to open the oven door a few times during the baking to let condensation out. The idea is to dry out the exterior of the meringues while keeping the inside moist.

PHOTOGRAPH ON PAGES 174–75 ➤

BLUEBERRY CHEESECAKE

SERVES: 8–10

PREP TIME: 20 MINS + CHILLING AND COOLING · COOK TIME: 45 MINS–1 HOUR

V

18 **graham crackers**

18 **gingersnaps**

6 tablespoons **unsalted butter**

2⅓ cups **cream cheese**

⅔ cup **superfine sugar**

2 teaspoons **lemon juice**

seeds from 1 **vanilla bean**

¾ cup **crème fraîche** or **sour cream**

½ cup thick **Greek yogurt**

3 extra-large **eggs**

BLUEBERRY TOPPING:

2 cups **blueberries**

2 teaspoons **cornstarch**

3 tablespoons **water**

 TIP

Cherries are always welcome on a cheesecake, as are cranberries. Add a teaspoon of almond extract to the cheesecake mixture for the cherry version, and finely grated orange zest for the cranberry version.

A rich, creamy cheesecake cut by a sharper fruit topping. Luxurious.

Preheat the oven to 325°F.

Crush the cookies to a fine powder in a food processor—you should have about 2 cups. Transfer them to a bowl. Melt the butter and pour it over the cookie crumbs, stirring to completely coat them.

Press the cookie mixture into the bottom of a deep 8-inch springform or loose-bottom cake pan, then put it into the refrigerator until firm.

Beat together the cream cheese, superfine sugar, lemon juice, and seeds scraped from the vanilla bean until creamy. Mix in the crème fraîche or sour cream and yogurt, then the eggs, and beat until smooth.

Spoon the filling over the chilled cookie crust. Smooth over the top and bake in the oven for 45 minutes or until the filling has set (it may need another 10 minutes).

Place the pan on a wire rack to cool completely, then run a small paring knife around the inside of the pan to help release the cheesecake and transfer to a serving plate.

Toss the blueberries in the cornstarch and put them in a small saucepan with the water. Heat while stirring until the blueberries are bubbling and start to break up. Let cool, then spoon over the top of the cheesecake.

BAKED APPLES

SERVES: 4

PREP TIME: 15 MINS · COOK TIME: 30–45 MINS

DF · V · Ve (WF · GF if gluten-free bread is used and mincemeat is checked)

4 medium **apples**, such as Pippin
or Braeburn

1 slice of stale **bread**, white or gluten-free

½ cup homemade or other good-quality
vegan **mincemeat**

a pinch of **sea salt**

custard or **heavy cream**, to serve
(optional)

Baked apples are easy and perfect for a chilly autumnal night. They deserve to be more fashionable than they are.

Preheat the oven to 350°F. Line a baking sheet with parchment paper.

Dig out the cores of the apples without going all the way through to the bottom, then place them on individual squares of aluminum foil, big enough to wrap the apples, on the lined baking sheet.

Tear the bread into pea-size pieces and mix with the mincemeat and salt. Pack the bread mixture into the apples. Bring the foil up and wrap it loosely around them, then bake in the oven for 30–45 minutes, until tender.

Serve with custard or heavy cream, if you want.

≡ ALTERNATIVE TOPPINGS ≡

Instead of mincemeat, the following work well as toppings:
- Raspberries, brown sugar, and bread crumbs, served with vanilla ice cream.
- Dried apricots, golden raisins, and dried sour cherries, plumped in red wine and sugar, drizzled with butter, and served with heavy cream.

JOSSY'S JEWELED RHUBARB & MANGO

SERVES: 4

PREP TIME: 20 MINS · COOK TIME: 1 HOUR

WF · GF · DF · V · Ve

10 early forced thin **champagne rhubarb stalks**

½-inch piece of **fresh ginger**

2 or 3 **star anise**

⅔ cup **cranberry juice**

juice of 2 **limes**

¼ cup **superfine sugar**

1 large or 2 small ripe **mangoes**

a few **mint leaves**, to decorate

This is a simple but sublime combination, which also looks beautiful. The appearance of the deep yellow mango with the clear pink rhubarb, and the combination of their contrasting flavors, is wonderful.

Preheat the oven to 340°F.

Slice the rhubarb across on the diagonal into 2-inch pieces. Peel the ginger and cut into thin mathsticks.

Arrange the rhubarb, ginger, and star anise in a wide ovenproof dish. Put the cranberry juice, lime juice, and sugar into a saucepan and bring to a boil, stirring until the sugar has dissolved. Boil rapidly for 2 minutes, then pour onto the rhubarb.

Cover the dish tightly with aluminum foil and put it on the center shelf of the oven for about 1 hour, until the rhubarb is soft. Remove the foil and let cool completely.

Cut the mango flesh off the pit, then peel them and slice into thin strips. Arrange the mango strips among the rhubarb, with the star anise dotted on top, then chill in the refrigerator. Decorate with mint leaves before serving.

BAKED ALASKA

SERVES: 8

PREP TIME: 15 MINS + FREEZING · COOK TIME: 5 MINS

V

3¾ cups **vanilla** or **strawberry ice cream** (or any favorite flavor)

1 (8-inch) round **sponge cake** (store-bought, or made using ¼ quantity of **Ben's Victoria Sponge**, see page 102)

4 **egg whites**, at room temperature

¼ teaspoon **cream of tartar**

1 cup **superfine sugar**

This is fun to make, easier than you would think, and will make your guests squeal with nostalgic delight.

Line an 8-inch-diameter bowl with plastic wrap.

Remove the ice cream of your choice from the freezer and let it soften slightly. Pack the ice cream into the bowl tightly to make a neat dome shape and cover with more plastic wrap. Place in the freezer for at least 3 hours.

Preheat the oven to 425°F. Place the sponge cake on a baking sheet lined with parchment paper and set aside.

Put the egg whites into a large clean bowl, and use an electric handheld mixer to whisk them into soft peaks. Add the cream of tartar, then gradually add the sugar. Whisk until stiff and glossy.

Remove the ice cream from the freezer and discard the top layer of plastic wrap. Dunk the bottom of the bowl into a sink of hot water for a second. Invert the bowl over the sponge and use the plastic wrap to help coax the ice cream from the bowl. Discard the plastic wrap and immediately cover the ice cream with the meringue. Use a knife to coax the meringue into peaks.

Bake in the oven for 5 minutes, until the peaks are golden.

Serve immediately!

≡ TIP ≡

To be sure the meringue does not slide off the sides of the ice cream as you assemble it, we find that the real trick is to have particularly stiff meringue and really cold ice cream.

CRÈME BRÛLÉE

SERVES: 4

PREP TIME: 20 MINS · COOK TIME: 30–40 MINS

WF · GF · V

2½ cups **heavy cream**

1 **vanilla bean**

6 **egg yolks**

¼ cup **superfine sugar**, plus
    4 tablespoons

Henry maintains that you can gauge the quality of any restaurant by one mouthful of its crème brûlée. Yet it's not particularly hard to make well, and is terrifically impressive when you do. This—together with its swoonsome creaminess—makes it a perfect Valentine's Day dessert, especially with the addition of heart-shape ramekins.

Preheat the oven to 300°F. Have ready 4 heart-shape or standard ramekins.

Pour the cream into a saucepan. Cut the vanilla bean in half lengthwise and scrape the seeds into the cream, also adding the empty pod.

Heat to just below boiling point, then remove from the heat and let the vanilla infuse for 10 minutes before discarding the empty pod.

Meanwhile, whisk the egg yolks together with the ¼ cup of sugar until the mixture is pale and thick. Add the infused cream. Stir well before pouring into the 4 ramekins.

Place the ramekins in a deep roasting pan. Fill the pan with water to come about halfway up the sides of the ramekins, then cover the pan tightly with aluminum foil and bake in the oven for 30–40 minutes or until the custard is set but still wobbly. Remove from the oven and let the custards cool without the foil covering. Chill in the refrigerator until ready to serve.

To make the brûléed top, sprinkle a tablespoon of sugar over each dessert (do them one at a time) and, using a kitchen blowtorch or hot broiler, heat the sugar until burned. Let the burned sugar shell set for 5 minutes before serving.

· ·

We are opposed to the fashionable habit of adding berries to crème brûlée. It interferes with the pure creaminess of the dish. However, if you must make variations, there are a few interesting flavors that work well:

• Indian: Use 4 crushed cardamom pods instead of the vanilla.

• Boozy: Add a shot of rum or brandy to the custard.

• Orange: Steep a couple of teaspoons of finely grated orange zest in the cream, with or without the vanilla bean.

• Thanksgiving: Add a little pumpkin puree and nutmeg. It works.

≡ TIP ≡

This dessert is perfect for making in advance. The custard can be made the day before and chilled in a pitcher overnight. You can bake the custard in the morning, then pull the ramekins out of the refrigerator at the end of dinner, brûlée them, and send them straight to the table.

PHOTOGRAPH ON PAGES 185–86 ➞

ROASTED QUINCE COMPOTE

SERVES 6–8
PREP TIME: 15 MINS · COOK TIME: APPROX. 1¾ HOURS
WF · GF · DF · V · Ve

3 **quinces**

1 **bay leaf**

1 large strip of **lemon peel**

½ a **vanilla bean**, split in half lengthwise

1 cup **water**

1¼ cups **granulated sugar**

Lovely with cheese after dinner, and much easier than making membrillo (a traditional Spanish quince paste boiled for hours). The compote also goes well with panna cotta and other creamy puddings, as well as on top of a good yogurt for breakfast.

Preheat the oven to 400°F.

Peel and quarter the quinces (don't worry about coring them until after they have been baked, when they are soft and easier to manage). Arrange them in a roasting pan large enough that they have a little room around them.

Add the bay leaf, lemon peel, and vanilla bean and cover with the water and sugar. Cover tightly with aluminum foil and bake for 1 hour.

Remove the foil, then reduce the heat to 340°F, toss the quinces in the juices, and put the pan back in the oven for another 35–40 minutes. The compote is ready when it is a deep pinky red and the sugar syrup is thick.

Remove the cores from the quince pieces when they have cooled and before you serve the compote.

TIP

Small pieces of the cooked quince can also be added to crisps (see pages 71 and 59), or thinly sliced on a tart.

MONT BLANC

SERVES: 6
PREP TIME: 10 MINS · COOK TIME: 2½ HOURS
WF · GF · V

3 **egg whites**

¼ teaspoon **salt**

1 teaspoon **vanilla extract**

1 cup **superfine sugar**

FILLING:

1 (15½-oz) can **sweetened chestnut puree**

1¼ cups **heavy cream**, lightly whipped

Chestnuts are the unsung heroes of the winter table. Their subtle but rich flavor is enhanced when sweetened and combined with vanilla. This is a traditional Euorpean pudding loved by the Italians and the French— it is named after their favorite mountain.

Preheat the oven to 250°F. Line 2 baking sheets with parchment paper.

Using an electric handheld mixer, beat the egg whites, salt, and vanilla on high speed until soft peaks form.

Add half the sugar to the frothy egg whites. Whisk until stiff, then add the remaining sugar. Whisk until smooth and glossy.

Portion out 6 large meringue disks about 1½ inches apart on the prepared baking sheets. Bake in the oven for about 2½ hours. Let cool on the baking sheets before peeling from the paper.

When ready to serve, spoon the chestnut puree over the meringues and top with lightly whipped cream.

TIP

Sweetened chestnut puree, made from candied chestnuts, is available in larger supermarkets, speciality food stores, and online. If you can't find it, you have a couple of options:
• Buy crystallized chestnuts (marrons glacés) and puree them with a little vanilla extract but no sugar.
• Make the puree from scratch. Buy fresh chestnuts, make a cut in each shell, and boil them in water for about 10 minutes. Peel off the shells and skins and process the chestnuts in a food processor. Add just enough heavy cream to form a paste. Then add confectioners' sugar and vanilla extract to taste.

ROASTED PEACHES

SERVES: 4

PREP TIME: 5 MINS · COOK TIME: 15 MINS

WF · GF · V (DF · Ve if heavy cream is omitted)

4 ripe **white** or **yellow peaches**

½ cup **white wine**

½ cup **superfine sugar**

heavy cream, to serve (optional)

Sometimes the best things are the simplest. Make sure you get the best peaches you can afford.

Preheat the oven to 425°F.

Halve the peaches and remove the pits. Arrange the peach halves in a roasting pan, cut side up. Add the white wine and sprinkle with the superfine sugar.

Bake in the oven for 12–15 minutes, until the fruit is a little golden on the edges and the syrup is bubbling. Serve with cream, if you want.

═ TIP ═

Use ripe delicious peaches. If they are underripe, no amount of cooking will be able to save them.

BAKING BASICS

FLOUR

The role of flour is to provide structure. The proteins in traditional flours react with water, producing gluten, the strands of which create a lattice in which air bubbles can be trapped, giving your baked goods "lightness." However, some people find gluten hard to digest. Recipes using gluten-free flours will be more cakelike, although this effect can often be offset to some degree by adding other structure providers, such as eggs or gums.

TRADITIONAL WHEAT FLOUR
Whole wheat or white; all purpose, cake, pastry, or bread

What is it? Ground wheat. Whole wheat is made from the whole grain: the endosperm (proteinous/starchy), the germ (proteinous and full of vitamins), and the bran (fibrous). Other types of wheat flour are made from only the starchy endosperm. All-purpose flour is used for general baking; it produces less gluten than bread flour, which is used to make bread. Pastry flour has less protein than all-purpose flour and cake flour even less. Self-rising flour is all-purpose flour with baking powder and salt added. Protein in wheat flour can differ between brands, so you may need to experiment and adjust the measurements slightly for the best results.

What is it good for? Almost anything in traditional baking.

Is it good for me? For a lot of people, no. Wheat has changed beyond recognition in the past 100 years, because farmers have selectively bred it from its naturally occurring forms to the extremely high-yielding grains that are produced today. These advances have done a lot to help feed a growing global population, but at a cost.

Incidences of celiac disease, a severe allergy to gluten, causes the immune system to attack the lining of the small intestine. It has been doubling every 15 years since the 1970s. Some people are also allergic to wheat (not just to the gluten it contains). In addition, wheat intolerance is a growing problem—a less catastrophic but still unpleasant reaction to modern wheat proteins that can leave you feeling heavy, tired, and listless. If you have a body that can cope with it, wheat is a wonderful thing. If not, there are alternatives.

SPELT FLOUR
Whole grain or white

What is it? Spelt is an ancient variety of wheat that has not been transformed by selective breeding.

What is it good for? You can use spelt as a substitute for wheat in many dishes. It is higher in protein than many wheat flours but lower in gluten, so it will not give you the superb risen baked goods that you can create with wheat flour. However, it has a delicious nutty flavor. We love spelt.

Is it good for you? People with wheat allergy and intolerance can generally dig into spelt without problems. Celiacs must avoid spelt because it contains gluten. Our own experience is that it doesn't give you that bloated sensation you get from traditional wheat.

RYE FLOUR
What is it? Rye comes from the same family of grasses as wheat. It originated in Eastern Europe, where it grows well in cold climates and in poor soil. It is dense and dark and contains little gluten.

What is it good for? For making traditional rye breads (see page 14). Also strongly flavored beers, vodka, and whiskey.

Is it good for you? Many people find it more palatable than wheat, because it has lower gluten levels and has been less intensively bred. It is high in vitamins and soluble fiber, and it has a lower glycemic load than many wheat and spelt breads, so it is less likely to lead to weight gain.

BUCKWHEAT FLOUR
What is it? Buckwheat is actually not a wheat at all. It is not even a grass. It is a fruit seed from the rhubarb family and similar to a sunflower seed. It is gluten free.

What is it good for? We use the flour to make pancakes, the flakes to make granola and porridge, and it can be used as a couscous substitute in its groat form. However, it will not provide enough structure to make breads unless you add eggs or xanthan gum. It can be used alongside other flours for interesting flavor and texture combinations.

Is it good for you? Yes. It is high in nutrients, especially manganese and magnesium, and it also provides vitamins, zinc, and a whole host of other goodies. It is sometimes called the "king of the healing grains."

GLUTEN-FREE FLOUR
What is it? Any flour that does not contain gluten. You can mix your own or choose store-bought types, which will generally be various blends of rice, potato, buckwheat, and bean and pea flours. They will often have added gluten substitutes, such as xantham gum.

What is it good for? If you want to avoid gluten, you can use it as a flour substitute in instances where the dish you are making does not need the strong structure that gluten provides. In this book, we use it in crisps, scones, cakes, tarts and bread.

Is it good for you? These flours will not contain gluten, but some are refined, so they will not necessarily be packed full of nutrients.

CORNMEAL
What is it? Coarsely ground dried corn, also known as polenta in Italy (as opposed to corn flour, a finely ground flour, and cornstarch, which is ground into a starchy white powder).

What is it good for? We use it to give body to cakes while avoiding wheat flour. It has a beautiful yellow color and a mild, sweet flavor.

Is it good for you? It is a relatively complex carbohydrate that also contains protein and some vitamins. It's a reasonable food—it won't make a superhero of you overnight, but it isn't bad for you either.

CHICKPEA (BESAN) FLOUR
What is it? Ground-up dried chickpeas.

What is it good for? We use it to add body to some gluten-free cakes. It is also good for thickening stews. It can be a little bitter, so we like to use it sparingly.

Is it good for you? Yes. It is gluten free and has a low glycemic load, so it won't set your sugar levels racing. Contains a good amount of protein and iron.

LEAVENERS & THICKENERS

. . . .

1. YEAST

A microorganism that converts the sugars in flour into carbon dioxide bubbles, thus putting air into the dough. It comes in many forms: fresh cakes (from speciality suppliers), active dry yeast, and instant (rapid-rise) yeast. We specify the type used in each recipe, but if you are substituting one for another, make sure you follow the instructions on the package.

2. BAKING SODA

A chemical compound with a slightly alkaline taste that reacts with acids to form carbon dioxide bubbles.

3. BAKING POWDER

A mixture of baking soda and an acid compound (typically cream of tartar) that reacts when moistened to produce carbon dioxide bubbles. Some baking powders use wheat as a "moisture absorption agent." You can buy gluten-free ones that do not.

4. ARROWROOT, CORNSTARCH

Starchy powders, which are useful for gluten-free binding and thickening.

5. XANTHUM GUM

A thickener/binder that can be used at low concentrations to thicken sauces. Often used to help give gluten-free breads and cakes structure.

6. EGG SUBSTITUTE

Also known as "egg replacer," it is used to replace eggs in sponges and cakes for vegans and people who are allergic to them. Gluten-free versions are available. Normally made of soy protein and potato starch. Not something we use often, but nice if you are baking for a vegan.

1.

2.

4.

5.

6.

FATS

Fats play many roles in baking. They add moistness and tenderness. They create barriers between layers of flour, letting crispy pastries develop. They help gluten stretch in bread, and stop things from sticking to pans.

1. UNSALTED BUTTER

What is it? A golden block of dairy goodness made from churning cream to concentrate the butterfat. It is an emulsion of butterfat (about 80%), water, and milk proteins. Unsalted butter is normally used in baking, having a sweeter flavor.

What is it good for? The most common baking fat, butter is solid at room temperature and can therefore be used to make all kinds of flaky pastries. It melts at body temperature, so it doesn't taste greasy.

Is it good for me? Along with suet (see opposite), butter is mostly saturated fat and is therefore high in calories. These foods used to be considered the devil's work, but they are all natural and recent nutritional research suggests that (within reason) they will probably do us less harm than processed alternatives. Because it is a saturated fat, butter can also be heated without changing its structure and becoming more harmful. Butter contains little lactose and is therefore rarely a problem for people with lactose intolerance.

2. SALTED BUTTER

What is it? Butter that has had salt added as a preservative and to change the flavor.

What is it good for? Generally we prefer the sweeter flavor of unsalted butter in baking and desserts. Occasionally the stronger flavor of salted butter gets the green light.

Is it good for me? Much the same as unsalted butter. If you need to watch your salt levels, choose unsalted butter.

3. COCONUT OIL

What is it? The oil extracted from coconut meat.

What is it good for? It is liquid at body temperature, but just about solid at room temperature. This makes it a possible substitute for butter in many applications (but, as you will see from the recipes, you must handle it differently). Its melting point (about 73°F) is much closer to room temperature than butter (about 90°F) or cocoa butter (about 93°F), which gives it unique qualities. Coconut oil frosting, for example, melts in the mouth differently than the richer buttercreams. (If you have ever tried Lindt Lindor chocolates—which contain a lot of coconut oil—you will recognize the sensation.)

Is it good for me? There is a great deal of debate over this. When people started cutting dairy out of their diet, coconut oil was seen as a perfect substitute. However, nutritionists pointed out that it was also high in calories and saturated fats. More recent evidence has shown that coconut oil promotes good cholesterol and that it is easily metabolized into fuel (rather than deposited as fat). Of course, this is only useful if you need the fuel. Our feeling is that it is a good fat; some people say it will make you chubby, but many nutritionists disagree. Read labels carefully, because some coconut oil is still hydrogenated. Always choose organic and unrefined.

4. OLIVE OIL

What is it? The oil extracted from olive flesh.

What is it good for? It is liquid at room temperature and therefore less versatile in baking than other fats discussed here. We use it in breads and pizza doughs and to toast granola.

Is it good for you? Yes. It is high in monounsaturated fats that may help protect against heart disease. It also contains a useful source of omega-6 fats, which we must eat because our bodies cannot make them from other foods. (Make sure you get the cold-pressed type.)

5. SUET

What is it? Raw beef (and sometimes sheep) fat, often taken from around the kidneys, also known as beef fat or kidney fat. It's available in large chunks or sometimes shredded from some butchers. You can replace it with shortening from a meat or vegetable source, but choose carefully—look for ones with reduced hydrogenated trans-fats.)

What is it good for? Making traditional English steamed puddings. The suet is hard and therefore forms hard pockets in the pastry. When the pudding is cooking, these melt away, leaving air pockets and a wonderful light, spongy texture.

Is it good for me? It is a high-calorie saturated fat. However, the link between saturated fat and heart disease is now under dispute, with recent studies pointing to manufactured trans-fats and sugary foods as the real villains. Therefore: Don't eat suet every day, but it's fine as an occasional treat.

6. LARD

What is it? Pig fat, often rendered (melted slowly), purified, and then reset.

What is it good for? Generally used to make really flaky pastries (for example, the hot water crust pastry used for the pork pie on page 42). It is solid at body temperature and has a distinct, soft porky flavor. We don't use it much.

Is it good for you? Very calorific, but probably not as sinful as its reputation would suggest. Eat it about as often as you would suet (see left).

7. MARGARINE

What is it? A butter substitute originally manufactured from beef fat but now more commonly made by thickening vegetable oils and dying them yellow.

What is it good for? Absolutely nothing. We don't think that any recipe tastes better when made with margarine.

Is it good for you? Traditional margarines, made from hydrogenating vegetable oil, were marketed as a healthier and cheaper alternative to butter. We now know that the manufacturing process created deadly trans-fats, and these types of marg have disappeared from the shelves. More recent manufacturing methods have produced a slew of products with their own advertised "health benefits." However, they have only recently entered the food chain and we would advise caution. Our general rule of thumb is: Avoid cooking with any ingredient that was invented in the last 1,000 years.

1.

3.

5.

4.

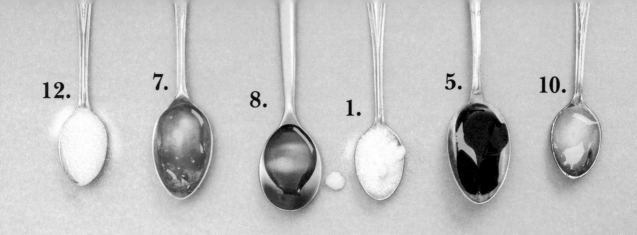

It is one of the tragedies of the human condition that sweet foods were not that commonplace when our palates were evolving. To early man, sugar was a rare and valuable source of energy. As a result, we have evolved to seek it out and wolf it down. Our tastebuds, which usually guide us toward things that are good for us, tell us that sweet things are to be gulped down with abandon.

Until as recent as the mid-eighteenth century, it was impossible to get hold of sugar in enough quantity to do us harm. However, white processed sugar is now cheap and plentiful, and over the last couple of decades it has been recognized (alongside processed carbohydrates) as the single greatest threat to our health. In the end, moderation is the answer, but there are some sweet substances out there that enable us to satisfy those evolutionary instincts while offering a little more protection to our bodies.

SUGAR

Sugar is made by distilling a sweet syrup—usually taken from sugarcane or sugar beet—until it crystallizes. It is almost irresistible. We try to use substitutes where possible. Where you do use it, here are a few rules:

Use canesugar (preferably Fairtrade), not beet sugar. Beet sugar has a funny taste, particularly noticeable in frostings.
Use unrefined sugar—it has a slightly nicer taste and at least retains some minerals and nutrients.
Eat only as a treat. Otherwise it will make your blood sugar soar and then slump, leaving you moody and, later, fatter.

Sugar comes in many forms from white superfine sugar or granulated sugar to dark brown muscovado. If you are ever on vacation in a sugar-producing country, take an afternoon off the beach to visit a sugar refinery. They are amazing places. The cane is ground by vast grooved metal rollers sprayed with hot water, and the resulting syrup is boiled to varying levels of darkness in bubbling vats. The smell is intoxicating. Unrefined sugars are spun off from the syrups at varying concentration levels (each darker than the last), using a centrifuge. The final remaining sweet syrup is called molasses, which is dense in nutrients compared to other sugars. Some sugars used frequently in baking are:

1. UNREFINED WHITE SUGAR

Unrefined means it contains molasses; refined sugar has this source of nutrients and flavor removed. Unrefined cane sugar comes from an early stage of distillation. The crystals are sold as granulated sugar or they are ground—which makes them easy to mix, melt, and dissolve—and sold as superfine sugar.

2. UNREFINED DEMERARA SUGAR

Darker than white sugar, with a stronger flavor. The larger crystals of this raw sugar give it a satisfyingly crunchy bite.

3. MUSCOVADO SUGAR

This sugar is not spun in the centrifuge, but is left to dry in the sun. It therefore contains more plant matter, which gives it a rich flavor. It is different from, and much nicer than, the typical brown sugar (which can be used as a substitute) that is made by adding molasses to white sugar.

4. CONFECTIONERS' SUGAR

Also known as powdered sugar, a finely ground refined white sugar that generally contains an anticaking agent.

5. MOLASSES (AND GOLDEN SYRUP)

The leftover syrup when the sugar crystals have been spun. Golden syrup, a light version used in British cooking, is made from the by-product of the first white sugar production; it is sold in large U.S. supermarkets (corn syrup is a substitute). Molasses (like dark treacle used in British cooking) is made from later boilings; it has more plant matter and less sugar.

6. FRUCTOSE

The sugar in cane sugar is sucrose, which is made up of glucose and fructose (the latter also occurs naturally in fruit). Sugar can be treated to create fructose, which is less likely to give you a sugar high followed by a sugar low. However, recent evidence suggests that it might turn to fat more easily than other sugars. In this book, we use other natural sweeteners.

NATURAL SWEETENERS

Natural sweeteners are generally used because they cause less of a sugar rush than traditional sugar and are less refined, containing more nutrients. They still come with some caveats.

7. HONEY

Flower nectar collected by bees.

What is good about it? Natural and delicious. Many forms are high in fructose and therefore create less of a sugar rush.

Any problems? Much mass-market honey is made by feeding the bees sugar syrup—and so is nutritionally identical to sugar.

8. MAPLE SYRUP

A syrup from the sap of maple trees.

What is good about it? Like honey, it is natural and delicious. **Any problems?** The sweetness comes mostly from sucrose, and therefore it carries the same health warnings as sugar.

9. AGAVE NECTAR

A syrup produced from the Mexican agave plant. It is sweeter than honey but less viscous.

What is good about it? It tastes good and is much less likely to give you a sugar rush.

Any problems? Due to massive recent demand, much of it is now heavily processed.

10. BROWN RICE SYRUP

This is derived by culturing cooked rice with enzymes from dried barley sprouts to break down the starches, which is then strained off and the resulting sweet liquid cooked.

What is good about it? It is a natural product that will not give you a sugar rush and does not contain fructose.

Any problems? It has a strong flavor. It has not been widely available for long, but so far it seems to be fairly harmless.

11. YACON SYRUP

A dark molasses-like syrup made from a Peruvian root.

What is good about it? Unlike agave syrup, the compounds providing the sweetness in yacon syrup pass through the body without being metabolized at all.

Any problems? It has a pretty strong flavor. As yet, no one has claimed that it is bad for you.

12. STEVIA

A mintlike herb that is sweet but contains no calories. It has been hailed as the potential solution to the sugar problem.

What is good about it? Sweet without an aftertaste and contains no calories. Will not give you a sugar rush.

Any problems? It used to be almost impossible to get hold of, but there is now an increasing number of products available.

BAKING WITH ALTERNATIVES

Baking with alternatives to wheat flour, butter, and white sugar is easier than you might think. Think of these alternatives not as replacement ingredients but as new ones to experiment with. If you don't like to do much experimentation in the kitchen, don't worry—we have already done most of the work for you. All tried and tested, and this is one situation where curiosity definitely won't kill the cat.

To be more experimental, try using these ingredients in your own recipes. You may need some good old-fashioned trial and error before they work out. To help you, here are some rules that will let you predict how they may behave.

Flours
Rice flour is a great alternative to wheat if used in conjunction with a little xanthan gum, which is a good stand-in for gluten. Without it, cakes can crumble a little too much. Rice flour has a slightly coarser texture than that of wheat flour. The finely ground rice has a crumbly texture that is similar to almond meal and different from the light texture of wheat flour. It lies somewhere between wheat flour and corn flour.

Although corn and oats are alright for some people, they are not suitable for everyone with a wheat and gluten intolerance. We have tried to include recipes for everyone. Store-bought gluten-free flour mixes are an easy way to take your favorite recipe and make it suitable for you.

Sweeteners
Wherever superfine sugar is called for, it is usually not just for sweetness but also for its structural qualities. For that reason, be cautious about using substitutes, such as granulated sugar, especially for cakes and meringues.

Agave nectar is a wonderful sweetener and much easier for our bodies to digest than sugar. It is also suitable for those who can't have sugar or honey. It takes longer to absorb into the bloodstream, too, so your blood sugar doesn't go haywire. We also love maple syrup, but make sure it is 100 percent pure.

Dairy & egg alternatives
Coconut oil is an exciting discovery, if you are staying away from dairy. It makes fantastic frosting (although you'll need to chill it, because it stays liquid at a lower temperature than butter). It also works well baked in some cakes.

If soy milk agrees with you, you'll find it great to bake with. Rice milk and coconut milk are good, too, but they are a little different in texture. We use cashew nut butter in our vanilla frosting, along with soy (or rice) milk and coconut oil, and the creamy texture is a dream.

Egg alternatives are easier to find than you might expect. A little ground flaxmeal or chia seed makes a great nutritional substitute. You can also use applesauce to get the right texture in cakes. Commercial egg replacers are usually just soy and potato starch, which are thickeners.

TECHNIQUES

* *

Although all the recipes in this book contain enough directions for you to dive straight in, what follows is intended as a kind of mini masterclass in baking techniques.

* *

1. GENERAL TIPS

Make notes

You never know when you will try an experiment that creates something wonderful. Get into the habit of having a pencil and paper on hand to jot down what you have done.

If you are substituting ingredients, be prepared to experiment a little

For example, if you use spelt flour in place of whole-wheat flour, or fructose instead of sugar, you will find that their properties are different. They will produce different textures, absorb different amounts of liquid, and so on. Don't let this put you off experimentation—just be aware of it and observe the results in case you want to tweak the recipes next time.

Measure everything out first

Chefs call this *mise en place*—literally, "put in place." It makes the whole process more ordered and enjoyable. If you are a man, there is a chance that you will forget this advice.

2. MIXING AND MEASURING

Accurate measuring

It is important to measure ingredients accurately. Dry ingredients in a measuring cup should be leveled with the back edge of a blunt knife, for example, and we've said when to first pack ingredients, such as brown sugar, before measuring.

To measure liquid ingredients, use a transparent measuring cup with easy-to-read measurement lines and position it on a level surface. Bend down so that your eye is level with the top surface of the liquid when checking it agains the line.

Sifting

Put the ingredients that you want to sift into a large sieve held over a bowl. Tip the sieve to an angle of 30 degrees and knock the lower edge repeatedly with a metal spoon or the back of a knife until everything has passed through. With confectioners' sugar, you might have to crush the last few balls through with the back of a spoon. Alternatively, you can use a standard flour sifter with a triggerlike handle.

Combining dry ingredients

Sometimes sifting is not necessary. If you don't mind lumps and only want to evenly distribute leavening agents or spices through a large quantity of flour, you can use a wire whisk.

Creaming

There are two ways to cream your butter and sugar. The recipes in this book will each say which one to use.

The traditional method—this method is slightly more painstaking but gives the lightest cakes. Mix the butter (softened) vigorously with the sugar (ideally with an electric mixer) to trap air. Then mix in the other ingredients gradually in the following order: eggs, then some flour, then some liquid, then the rest of the flour, then the rest of the liquid.

The two-stage mixing method—the more common method in this country—produces soft but slightly heavier cakes. It is quicker. Mix all the dry ingredients in one bowl, then mix the butter into them (as if making a dough) before adding the wet ingredients until incorporated.

Folding

This is how you mix two semiliquid substances while preserving the air trapped in one of them (for example, melted chocolate and whisked egg, or fruit puree and whipped cream). We were taught slightly different ways to fold, but the principle remains the same—do it gently and without any obviously "crushing" or "deflating" motions.

Claire's method: Use a rubber spatula to gently but quickly fold together aerated eggs or cream with other ingredients. Swirls will form in the mixture but don't worry about mixing until they are gone, because you run the risk of overmixing.

Henry's method: Put the mixture with the air in it on top of the other mixture in a large bowl. Take a large metal spoon and cut vertically down into the middle of the bowl. When you hit the bottom, scoop the spoon around toward you, gently lifting the mixture and folding it back on top of the bowl. Rotate the bowl by 45 degrees and repeat until mixed.

3. PASTRY DOUGH—THE BASICS

General tips

When making most doughs, the trick is to trap little pieces of butter within a dough, which melt when you cook it and create something flaky and delicious as the water from the butter evaporates and turns to steam, which rises, pushing up the layers. Unless otherwise stated, therefore, make sure that all your ingredients are cold and that you make it in a cold room (if the butter melts before you cook it, you will get a dense result instead of a light and flaky one).

Always rest a dough in the refrigerator for at least half an hour before rolling it out. This allows for the gluten to relax, which will make the task much easier.

When rolling out dough for a tart pan, lift the pressure as you get to the edge of the dough to avoid making it too thin.

Your final pastry will vary depending on the type of flour you use, the fats, the humidity, the temperature, and so on. If you are eager to perfect the art, observe closely what happens each time you make a certain type of pastry and take notes. Over time, you will learn when an extra splash of water or a sift of flour are required.

Types of pastry doughs

The main three pastry doughs in this book are for making basic pie dough, flaky dough, and pat-in-pan dough. Flaky dough has thin layers of fat separating thin layers of dough and will break into thin flakes. Basic pie dough and pat-in-pan dough crumble into small pieces, because the fat has been worked through the flour. We provide recipes for these with the main recipes as appropriate, but thought it would be useful to give the basics here for easy reference—see the next page.

Henry thinks life is a little too short to be making your own puff pastry dough—you can now buy some good all-butter versions from the grocery store.

BASIC PIE DOUGH

MAKES: ONE 9-INCH CRUST

1⅔ cups **all-purpose flour**
a pinch of **salt**
5 tablespoons **unsalted butter**, cut
  into coarse ⅜-inch cubes
2½ tablespoons cold **water**

Sift the flour and salt and add the butter. Rub the mixture gently between your fingertips until it resembles coarse sand.

Sprinkle the water over the mixture and mix until it forms a cohesive ball of dough.

Wrap the dough in plastic wrap and let rest in the refrigerator for at least 30 minutes before using.

PAT-IN-PAN DOUGH

MAKES: ONE 8–9-INCH CRUST

1 cup plus 2 tablespoons **all-purpose flour**
2 tablespoons **superfine sugar**
7 tablespoons **unsalted butter**, melted
1 tablespoon **distilled white vinegar**

Blend the ingredients briefly in a food processor and pat into a tart pan.

FLAKY DOUGH

Use the same ingredients as the basic pie dough above but keep the pieces of butter larger and don't mix them in all the way.

4. EGGS

Buying eggs

Choose a decent-size free-range or pasture-raised egg. Chickens that are well fed and cared for produce yolks that are more yellow and lustrous. The yellow or orange yolks are also indicative of the seasons, because the greener the grass that the chickens are eating, the deeper the color of the yolks.

Storing eggs

Eggs are generally stored in the refrigerator. Consider transferring them to an airtight container to keep out smells from other foods, which can permeate the shells.

Bringing eggs to temperature

When baking, eggs should be at room temperature. If you forget to remove them from the frigerator with enough time to bring to room temperature, you can plunge them into warm water for a couple of minutes to speed up the process.

Breaking eggs

Break the shells against a flat worktop instead of against the edge of the bowl or with a knife or spoon. By using this method, there is less of a chance that pieces of shell will be forced into the egg.

Separating eggs

Holding the two halves of the broken egg above a bowl, move the yolk from one half shell to the other, back and forth, until all the white has fallen into the bowl. Then drop the yolk into another, smaller bowl. (If the yolk starts to break up, move fast and get the yolk into the yolks bowl. It is better to have a little white in the yolks bowl than a little yolk in the whites bowl. Yolk contamination makes it harder, if not impossible, to whisk the whites to soft peaks, see below.)

Whisking egg whites

This is one of the few cases where fresher is not better. It is actually slightly easier to whisk the whites of older, runnier eggs. MAKE SURE THE BOWL AND THE WHISK ARE CLEAN. Even just a little dirt—particularly fat, which can be found in egg yolks—can prevent a good voluminous cloud of whites. A pinch of salt or cream of tartar helps the whisking. Be careful not to overwhisk egg whites: once they have formed stiff peaks, additional whisking will cause them to break down.

QUICK CUSTARD

MAKES: 2½ CUPS
PREP TIME: 5 MINS · COOK TIME: 15 MINS
WF · GF · V

1 **vanilla bean**, split lengthwise

2 cups **heavy cream**

scant ½ cup **milk**

¾ cup **superfine sugar**

5 **egg yolks**, at room temperature

a pinch of **sea salt**

By using more cream than in most recipes, and—critically—heating the sugar with the cream instead of adding it to the egg yolks, this recipe avoids the nervous stage of heating the custard over the stove and waiting for it to thicken—or, more often than not, scramble.

Put the vanilla bean into a saucepan with the cream, milk, and superfine sugar. Bring to a boil, stirring to make sure the sugar dissolves. Remove the pan from the heat and let sit for 5 minutes.

Meanwhile, put the egg yolks into a blender and blend for 2 minutes, or until they become creamy. Add a small pinch of salt.

Bring the cream back to a boil, remove the vanilla bean, and pour the mixture slowly into the eggs, blending as you do so. Assuming that the cream is hot and the eggs not too cold, you should have a great not-too-thick custard. (If you want to make it thicker, heat it gently on the stove, but you shouldn't need to.)

5. MAKING CAKES

Here are some tips to help you avoid common errors when making cakes.

Creaming butter & eggs to avoid curdling

To help avoid curdling, always bring your ingredients to room temperature before you start. Your butter should be especially soft. Whip the butter and sugar together with an electric mixer. It is much easier than doing it by hand, and you will get enough air into the mixture to be able to hold the eggs. The butter and sugar mixture is ready when it has doubled in volume and turned almost white.

Add the eggs one by one, fully incorporating each addition.

If you're making a cake that has a lot of eggs (such as a sponge), add a teaspoon or two of flour to help stabilize the mixture, but not too much or the cake may become tough.

Slow & low

If in doubt when making a cake, bake it slow and low for greater moistness throughout. The name of this method came from a rap song that Claire is particularly fond of. "Slow and low that is the tempo" is the lyric, and it has become her baking mantra.

Avoiding domed cakes

There are two main reasons why cakes sometimes dome up in the middle.

(a) The metal on the outside of the pan conducts the heat faster. The sides of the cake set while the center still continues to bake and rise.

(b) The structure of the cake is too strong, preventing the leavening gases from escaping until toward the end of baking, when they erupt through the center in little tunnels. The batter may have been mixed too much after the flour was added, and the air bubbles try to escape through the middle. When glutens form, the crumb becomes dry and tough.

Avoiding sunken cakes

If a cake has baking soda in it and no acid (such as cream of tartar) to neutralize it, it can rise at first and then fall down. (Note: If a recipe calls for baking powder and you do not have any available, a mixture of baking soda and cream of tartar can be substituted.)

Always check the expiration dates on your leavening powders. They don't last forever, and expired leavening powders are the source of many failed cakes.

Too much batter in the cake pan can cause a cake to sink in the middle. When baking a sponge, always leave about one-quarter of the pan unfilled to give the cake room to rise up. Fruitcakes won't rise as much, so you can fill the pan more. Sinking can also be a sign that your cake is underbaked.

Try not to rush the cooling of a cake. As cake cools, it continues to bake slightly. Rushing it might mean it sinks.

To test for doneness

There are three ways to test for doneness.

The toothpick method: Good for denser cakes. Insert a toothpick (or a long thin knife) into the center of the cake, and when it pulls out clean, the cake is done.

The listening method: Henry's mother-in-law, Petra (see page 114), swears by this for fruitcakes. Open the oven door, remove the cake, and listen. A fruitcake will "hiss" gently as it cooks, or as Petra says "sings." When it stops singing, it is done.

The pressing method: Good for lighter cakes, such as sponges. Press down gently on the top of the cake; when it springs back instead of leaving a slight dent, it is done.

Be sure to use the right method, because not every method works for every cake. Some cakes are meant to be moist, so the toothpick test isn't foolproof. The spring-back-to-the-touch test is not sufficient if a cake is supposed to be soft. The "listening" method works best for fruitcakes, and the timer is never to be trusted.

Convection ovens

Often cookbooks will ask you to put the cake in the middle of the oven, because heat rises and the top can be hotter than the bottom. Modern convection ovens are efficient at circulating heat evenly around the oven with a fan, so there's no need to worry about positioning.

Even if you have a few racks filled, the heat will be pushed by the fan all around the baking cakes.

However, not everyone has a convection oven. All the recipes in this book have been tested without a fan, with the cakes positioned on the middle shelf of the oven. If you are using a convection oven, reduce the given temperature by 25°F or according to the oven manufacturer.

6. DOUGH

Kneading

When kneading dough by hand, remember that you are trying to stretch the gluten. This requires energy. Henry likes to break a sweat when making and baking bread.

He says if you are not breaking a sweat, you are not working it hard enough. Big long stretches with the ball of the hand are the thing. Claire is a fan of the slap-and-tickle method: stretching the dough up and out, then slapping it down onto a work surface instead of using the pushing method.

The idea with this method is to incorporate air into the dough while kneading and to form the gluten so that you don't need to add as much flour to the bread. Both methods will produce equally beautiful bread.

7. FROSTINGS

There are three main types of frostings that we use in this book: basic icing, buttercream, and royal icing.

Basic icing is a mixture of water (or fruit juice or puree) and confectioners' sugar that forms a delicate, flat crispy coating when set.

Royal icing is similar to a basic icing, but it uses egg white to make it harden to a much more brittle texture.

Buttercream is a rich and creamy mixture of sugar, butter, and flavouings. Claire has also come up with a vegan version of buttercream using coconut oil, soy milk, and agave nectar.

You can find recipes for frostings on the following pages:

8. STORING

Cakes, bread & cookies
These should all be wrapped in wax paper and put into an airtight container at room temperature. Storing them in the refrigerator will make them turn stale more quickly (starches crystallize faster at colder temperatures). Bread freezes well. Try slicing it and storing it in airtight bags, then toasting it straight from the freezer.

Baking ingredients
Any ingredients that live in the refrigerator are best kept in an airtight container to stop them from picking up the smells of other foods. It's also best to store flour, sugar, and other dry pantry ingredients in airtight containers to keep out any moisture.

Sterilizing jars
To sterilize clean, washed, and dried jars or bottles, put them into a cold oven with the lids off. Turn the oven on to 340°F and put the timer on for 20 minutes. When the bell goes, turn off the oven, leaving the jars inside. Pour in your preserves, jelly, chutney, or syrup while the jars are still hot.

9. SUBSTITUTES

Substitutes for buttermilk
Buttermilk and yogurt make cakes soft and moist because of their acidity. If you don't have buttermilk, you can use half the quantity of plain yogurt mixed with half the quantity of whole milk. Another alternative is to use 1 tablespoon of fresh lemon juice with ¾ cup plus 2 tablespoons milk—this will make almost 1 cup of buttermilk.

Substitutes for sugars
If you have run out of brown sugar, you can add 1 tablespoon of molasses (or black treacle) to 1 cup of superfine or granulated sugar to get a similar flavor.

If you don't have Demerara sugar, you can use light brown sugar as a substitute.

INDEX

ABOUT THE AUTHORS

CLAIRE PTAK is former Pastry Chef at the legendary California restaurant Chez Panisse, and now chef-proprietor of Violet Cakes in London. She was chosen to make Prince Harry and Meghan Markle's wedding cake. Claire hosts Violet Sessions, a podcast that explores culture, creativity, work, and lifestyle through conversations with fascinating women. She is author of *The Violet Bakery Cookbook, The Home-Made Sweet Shop, Sweets, Candy & Chocolates, The Whoopie Pie Book,* and *LEON Baking & Puddings.*

HENRY DIMBLEBY is cofounder of healthy fast food chain, LEON. With John Vincent and Allegra McEvedy, the first branch was opened in London in July 2004, and six months after opening, LEON was named the Best New Restaurant in Great Britain at the *Observer Food Monthly* Awards.

LEON now has more than 60 restaurants (including branches in Washington, D.C., Amsterdam, Utrecht, and Oslo). The first LEON cookbook was published in 2008 and a decade on, the range now includes 15 titles.

To George, Johnny, and Dory for their unshakeable conviction that I am the best cook in the world. And to my wife, Mima, who makes everyone around her feel they have so much to give. —HD

For Damian and Shuggie.—CP

An Hachette UK Company
www.hachette.co.uk

First published in Great Britain in 2019 by
Conran Octopus Limited, an imprint of
Octopus Publishing Group Ltd
Carmelite House
50 Victoria Embankment
London EC4Y 0DZ
www.octopusbooks.co.uk
www.octopusbooksusa.com

Distributed in the USA by
Hachette Book Group
1290 Avenue of the Americas
4th and 5th Floors
New York, NY 10104

Distributed in Canada by
Canadian Manda Group, 664 Annette St.
Toronto, Ontario, Canada M6S 2C8

Except for the recipes on pages 128–129, 142–143, 160–161, and 164–165, the recipes in this book were previously published in *Leon Baking & Puddings*.

ISBN 978 1 84091 798 7

Printed and bound in China

10 9 8 7 6 5 4 3 2 1

Publisher: Alison Starling
Assistant Editor: Emily Brickell
Creative Director: Jonathan Christie
Design: Ella McLean
Senior Production Manager: Katherine Hockley

Special Photography: Steven Joyce
(Photography on pages 204 and 223: Georgia Glynn Smith)
Food styling: Sian Henley
Food styling assistants: Grace Evans, Anna Hiddlestone, and Libby Silbermann
Prop styling: Lauren Law

All the recipes in this book have been tested without a fan, with the cakes positioned on the middle shelf of the oven. If you are using a convection oven, reduce the given temperature by 25°F or follow the oven manufacturer's directions.